ISBN 978-0-243-93600-7
PIBN 10805578

1 MONTH OF
FREE
READING

at

www.ForgottenBooks.com

By purchasing this book you are eligible for one month membership to ForgottenBooks.com, giving you unlimited access to our entire collection of over 700,000 titles via our web site and mobile apps.

To claim your free month visit: www.forgottenbooks.com/free805578

English
Français
Deutsche
Italiano
Español
Português

www.forgottenbooks.com

Mythology Photography **Fiction**
Fishing Christianity **Art** Cooking
Essays Buddhism Freemasonry
Medicine **Biology** Music **Ancient
Egypt** Evolution Carpentry Physics
Dance Geology **Mathematics** Fitness
Shakespeare **Folklore** Yoga Marketing
Confidence Immortality Biographies
Poetry **Psychology** Witchcraft
Electronics Chemistry History **Law**
Accounting **Philosophy** Anthropology
Alchemy Drama Quantum Mechanics
Atheism Sexual Health **Ancient History**
Entrepreneurship Languages Sport
Paleontology Needlework Islam
Metaphysics Investment Archaeology
Parenting Statistics Criminology
Motivational

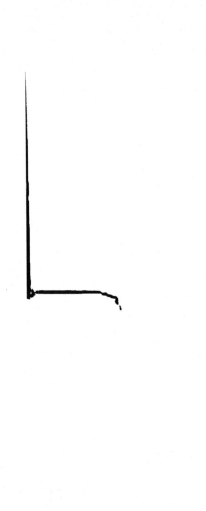

MILTON

ON THE SON OF GOD AND
THE HOLY SPIRIT

MILTON

on

The Son of God

and

The Holy Spirit

FROM HIS TREATISE

On Christian Doctrine

WITH INTRODUCTION BY
ALEXANDER GORDON, M.A.

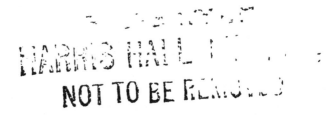
London
BRITISH & FOREIGN UNITARIAN ASSOCIATION
ESSEX HALL, ESSEX STREET, STRAND W.C.
1908

PRINTED BY ELSOM AND CO., HULL

INTRODUCTION

In the sixth volume (published 1880) of his *Life of John Milton*, the late Professor Masson writes : 'Two of his manuscripts about which, as we know, he was especially anxious just before his death [which occurred on 8 November, 1674] were the small one containing the fair transcript of his *Latin Letters of State* and the much larger one containing that complete *Treatise of Christian Doctrine* or *Systematic Body of Divinity*, on which he had so long been engaged.' These manuscripts were left by Milton 'to the charge of the young scholar, Daniel Skinner, B.A., of Trinity College, Cambridge, who had for some time been his amanuensis'; apparently 'on the understanding that Skinner would do his best to have the two books printed in Holland.' On 20 November, 1676, Daniel Elzevir writes to Sir Joseph Williamson, Secretary of State, that about a year before he had agreed with Skinner to print both manuscripts, but having found 'things which I judged fitter to be suppressed than published, I resolved to print neither the one nor the other.' On 19 February, 1677, he writes to Skinner's father, a London merchant, stating that he will send him the manuscripts, to be placed in Williamson's hands. They came to London in a parcel addressed *To Mr. Skinner, mercht*; the parcel was put into a press in the old State Paper Office in Whitehall; and there, in the latter part of 1823, this parcel was discovered by Robert Lemon, the deputy-keeper, among papers of 1677, 1678, and 1683.

By command of George IV, the editing of the treatise *De Doctrina Christiana* was entrusted to his then librarian and historiographer, Charles Robert Sumner, afterwards successively bishop of Llandaff (1826) and Winchester (1827). In 1825 Sumner published simultaneously the Latin treatise, and an English translation (revised by William Sidney Walker, a classic scholar of high rank, and a well-known Shakespearean critic). The Latin original was reprinted at Brunswick in 1827. The English translation was reproduced at Boston, Mass., in 1825 (giving rise to Channing's remarkable *Essay on Milton*); it was also included in the fourth and fifth volumes (1853) of the edition of Milton's Prose Works in Bohn's Standard Library.

Though thus placed ' before the world, it seems to have found few real readers,' writes Masson. Yet he adds that 'it is not to be overlooked or dismissed carelessly. Not only does it throw

light upon *Paradise Lost,* not only does it form
an indispensable commentary to some obscure
parts of that poem by presenting in explicit
and categorical prose what is there imaginatively
assumed and even veiled; but it tells us a good
deal about Milton and his opinions besides,
peculiarly and even oddly characteristic, that
we should not have known otherwise, or should
have known but vaguely.'

To this neglect of Milton's own exposition
of his ultimate views on theology, we must
ascribe the attempts which from time to time
have been made to identify him with opinions
which he decisively rejected.

In 1679, Titus Oates, dedicating to the King
his *True Narrative of the Horrid Plot,* etc., asserts
that ' Milton was a known frequenter of a Popish
Club.' In 1684, Thomas Long, in his *Com-
pendious History of all the Popish and Fanatical
Plots,* etc., affirms that ' Milton was by very
many suspected to be a Papist, and if Dr. Oates
may be believed, was a known frequenter of the
Popish Club, though he were Cromwell's Secretary.' Milton's younger brother, Christopher,
was deputy-recorder of Ipswich at the time of
the poet's death. Later than this, according to
his biographer (Mr. J. M. Rigg, in *Dict. Nat.
Biog.*) ' he was, or professed to be, a Roman
Catholic, and accordingly, though no great law-
yer, was raised by James II to the Exchequer

bench, 26 April, 1686, being first invested with
the coif (21 April), and knighted (25 April). His
tenure of office was equally brief and undis-
tinguished. On 16 April, 1687, he was transferred to the Common Pleas, and on 6 July, 1688,
he was discharged as superannuated [he was in
his seventy-third year], retaining his salary.'
Now Sir John Perceval (1683–1748), afterwards
Earl of Egremont, writes in his autobiography
that Dr. Arthur Charlett told him [some time
after 1699] that he had heard from Dr. Wm.
Binckes, that Binckes was 'at an entertainment
in King James' reign, when Sir Christopher
Milton . . . did then say publicly his brother
was a Papist some years before he died, and
that he died so.' Further, Perceval writes that
Dr. English told him that 'he had often heard
Mr. Prior, the poet, say that the late Earl of
Dorset told him the same thing.' Thus Perceval
gives us, at fourth hand, but along two lines,
the ascription to Sir Christopher Milton of a
statement which is evidently false ; for its utterance not even the atmosphere of an 'entertainment' could furnish any valid excuse. Perceval's
statement was first published in 1879, in the
Seventh Report of the Historical Manuscripts
Commission.

Not till this present year did any persons
venture to treat this story as furnishing serious
evidence that Milton had preceded his brother as

a convert to the Church of Rome. This fatuity has been adventured by Mr. W. H. Grattan Flood, in the *Tablet* (23 May, 1908), and by Monsignor A. S. Barnes, himself a convert, in the *Cambridge Review* (10 June, 1908). The latter fixes the ' entertainment ' as being an Assize Dinner at Warwick, and this on the strength of a passage, and a note, in Dr. Binckes' printed sermon of 5 Nov. 1704. Here, however, Binckes does not say that he had himself heard Sir Christopher Milton's statement. Monsignor Barnes, while too good a stickler for antiquity to attach any weight to a publication that did not appear till 1825, bases his case on the sermon of 1704, and the publication of 1879. It may suffice to note, that in his treatise *On Christian Doctrine* Milton denies that ' any preference was given ' to Peter ' over the other apostles '; says that the text, Matt. xvi. 18, 19, ' is perverted by the Pope to form the charter of his authority '; repudiates transubstantiation (which he calls ' anthropophagy, for it deserves no better name ') and ' the Mass of the Papists,' as involving ' a profanation too horrible to be even alluded to without shuddering '; maintains that ' the privilege of dispensing the elements is confined to no particular man or order of men '; rejects ' the fable of a purgatory ' which ' the Papists feign '; and more to the same purpose. In the *Belfast Newsletter* this autumn a correspondence respecting Milton's religious standing ran a singular course. No one invoked the authority of Titus Oates or of Monsignor Barnes. Nor did it appear that the writers (with two exceptions) were in a position to quote from the work which Masson rightly treats as Milton's own key to his religious position. Milton was claimed as an Anglican (whereas he was an Independent); and as a Trinitarian, on the strength of isolated passages, especially from his earlier writings, interpreted in accordance with the wishes of the respective writers. There is no doubt that Milton's writing, both in poetry and prose, exhibits a movement of theological opinion, continuous from his early days; for his was no stagnant mind. *Paradise Regained* even exhibits this movement as compared with *Paradise Lost.* For the deliberate and reasoned views which he ultimately reached, recourse must needs be had to his treatise *On Christian Doctrine.* This treatise, as Sumner observes, is ' distinguished in a remarkable degree by calmness of thought, as well as by moderation of language.'

Masson well says that ' Milton's fundamental idea in the treatise is that . . . . though every sane man must be naturally a theist, yet no one can have right thoughts of God by natural reason alone, and the condition of mankind as respects matters supernatural would have been that of almost

complete agnosticism, but for the divine revelation contained in the Christian Scriptures. The
divine origin and inspiration of these Scriptures,
defined as comprising only and precisely those
books of the Old and New Testaments which
Protestants have accepted as canonical, is Milton's
assumption throughout.' Masson remarks that
this assumption Milton does not think it necessary to prove ; and accounts for the omission
on the ground that Milton wrote as a believer
for believers. Milton, however, does not lie open
to this criticism quite so palpably as Masson
implies. He distinguishes between the authen-
ticity of the books in question—which, he holds,
may be established, as that of others cannot, by
external testimony confirmed by internal evidence
—and their binding authority, respecting which
he says (almost quoting the Westminster Confession) ' the truth of the entire volume is established
by the inward persuasion of the Spirit working
in the hearts of individual believers.' He further,
with many Puritans, as well as Quakers, maintains
that while ' the written word is highly important,'
yet ' the external Scripture ' may be, and has
been, corrupted ; whereas ' the Spirit that leads
to truth cannot be corrupted.'

On the basis of Scripture, then, to the exclusion
of ecclesiastical tradition and conciliar decisions
—though not disdaining all help of commentators
(his favourite is Beza), or of patristic writers,

whose opinions he frequently commends—Milton constructs his system; which includes in its two books (the first consisting of thirty-three, the second of seventeen chapters) not merely theology proper, but church order, and public and private duty.

In every Christian theology the Christology is a matter of supreme interest. Hence Sumner rightly advises any who are in doubt 'as to the real sentiments of Milton respecting the second person of the Trinity,' to study the fifth chapter of the first book, *Of the Son of God*. He very fairly condenses its purport thus: 'It is there asserted that the Son existed in the beginning, and was the first of the whole creation; by whose delegated power all things were made in heaven and earth; begotten, not by natural necessity, but by the decree of the Father, within the limits of time; endued with the divine nature and substance, but distinct from and inferior to the Father; one with the Father in love and unanimity of will, and receiving everything, in his filial as well as in his mediatorial character, from the Father's gift.'

This chapter, and the one which follows it, *Of the Holy Spirit*, are here reprinted in full, from the second edition (1853) of Sumner's translation.

Sumner adds that, on the Vicarious Atonement, Milton's views leave 'nothing to be desired.'

This doctrine is exhibited at length in the three chapters *Of Man's Restoration, and of Christ as Redeemer, Of the Functions of the Mediator, and of his Threefold Office, Of the Ministry of Redemption.* It was the argument, not only of Milton, but of those who, like Dr. Samuel Clarke in the eighteenth century, held a kindred view of the person of Christ, that on their system ' Christ's death was real,' as Milton puts it ; which it could not have been, he affirms, on the system of ' those who consider the Son as of the same essence with the Father.'

Milton does not employ the expression Original Sin. At the same time he holds, on the one hand, that all mankind did sin in Adam, and have thence incurred a moral deterioration ; on the other hand, that ' no one perishes, except he himself sin,' by a personal act of his own. On Predestination he endeavours to take a middle course, securing the freedom of the human will, while maintaining the Divine foreknowledge. In regard to eternal punishment his mind seems not absolutely made up. It ' varies with the degree of guilt.' With Chrysostom and Luther he thinks it probable that hell is situated, not at the centre of the earth, but ' beyond the limits of this universe.' For, ' if as has been shown from various passages of the New Testament, the whole world is to be finally consumed by fire, it follows that hell, being situated in the centre of the earth, must share the fate of the surrounding universe, and perish likewise ; a consummation more to be desired than expected by the souls in perdition.'

In his *Dedication*, addressed *To all the Churches of Christ, and to all who profess the Christian Faith throughout the World*, Milton says, ' If I communicate the result of my inquiries to the world at large ; if, as God is my witness, it be with a friendly and benignant feeling towards mankind, that I readily give as wide a circulation as possible to what I esteem my best and richest possession, I hope to meet with a candid reception from all parties, and that none at least will take unjust offence, even though many things should be brought to light which will at once be seen to differ from certain received opinions. I earnestly beseech all lovers of truth, not to cry out that the Church is thrown into confusion by that freedom of discussion and inquiry which is granted to the schools, and ought certainly to be refused to no believer, since we are ordered *to prove all things*, and since the daily progress of the light of truth is productive far less of disturbance to the Church, than of illumination and edification.'

' For my own part,' he adds, ' I adhere to the Holy Scriptures alone—I follow no other heresy or sect. I had not even read any of the works of heretics, so called, when the mistakes of those

who are reckoned for orthodox, and their in-
cautious handling of Scripture, first taught me to
agree with their opponents whenever those opponents agreed with Scripture.   If this be heresy,
I confess with St. Paul, Acts xxiv. 14, *that after
the way which they call heresy, so worship I the
God of my fathers, believing all things which are
written in the law and the prophets*—to which
I add, whatever is written in the New Testament.   Any other judges or paramount interpreters of the Christian belief, together with all
implicit faith, as it is called, I, in common with
the whole Protestant Church, refuse to recognize.'

A. G.

VICTORIA PARK, MANCHESTER,
    30 *October*, 1908.

JOHN MILTON

BORN 9 DECEMBER 1608
DIED 8 NOVEMBER 1674

THE SON OF GOD

PREFATORY REMARKS

I CANNOT enter upon subjects of so much difficulty as the SON OF GOD and the HOLY SPIRIT, without again premising a few introductory remarks. If indeed I were a member of the Church of Rome, which requires implicit obedience to its creed on all points of faith, I should have acquiesced from education or habit in its simple decree and authority, even though it denies that the doctrine of the Trinity, as now received, is capable of being proved from any passage of Scripture. But since I enrol myself among the number of those who acknowledge the Word of God alone as the rule of faith, and freely advance what appears to me much more clearly deducible from the Holy Scriptures than the commonly received opinion, I see no reason why anyone who belongs to the same Protestant or Reformed Church, and professes to acknowledge the same rule of faith as myself, should take

B

offence at my freedom, particularly as I impose my authority on no one, but merely propose what I think more worthy of belief than the creed in general acceptation. I only entreat that my readers will ponder and examine my statements in a spirit which desires to discover nothing but the truth, and with a mind free from prejudice. For without intending to oppose the authority of Scripture, which I consider inviolably sacred, I only take upon myself to refute human interpretations as often as the occasion requires, conformably to my right, or rather to my duty as a man. If indeed those with whom I have to contend were able to produce direct attestation from heaven to the truth of the doctrine which they espouse, it would be nothing less than impiety to venture to raise, I do not say a clamour, but so much as a murmur against it. But inasmuch as they can lay claim to nothing more than human powers, assisted by that spiritual illumination which is common to all, it is not unreasonable that they should on their part allow the privileges of diligent research and free discussion to another inquirer, who is seeking truth through the same means and in the same way as themselves, and whose desire of benefiting mankind is equal to their own.

In reliance, therefore, upon the divine assistance, let us now enter upon the subject itself.

OF THE SON OF GOD

Hitherto I have considered the INTERNAL EFFICIENCY of God, as manifested in his decrees.

His EXTERNAL EFFICIENCY, or the execution of his decrees, whereby he carries into effect by external agency whatever decrees he has purposed within himself, may be comprised under the heads of GENERATION, CREATION, and the GOVERNMENT OF THE UNIVERSE.

First, GENERATION, whereby God, in pursuance of his decree, has begotten his only Son; whence he chiefly derives his appellation of Father.

Generation must be an external efficiency, since the Father and Son are different persons; and the divines themselves acknowledge this, who argue that there is a certain emanation of the Son from the Father (which will be explained when the doctrine concerning the Holy Spirit is under examination); for though they teach that the Spirit is co-essential with the Father, they do not deny its emanation, procession, spiration, and issuing from the Father,—which are all expressions denoting external efficiency. In conjunction with this doctrine they hold that the Son is also co-essential with the Father, and generated from all eternity. Hence this question, which is naturally very obscure, becomes involved in still greater difficulties if the received opinion respecting it be followed; for

though the Father be said in Scripture to have
begotten the Son in a double sense, the one
literal, with reference to the production of the
Son, the other metaphorical, with reference to
his exaltation, many commentators have applied
the passages which allude to the exaltation and
mediatorial functions of Christ as proof of his
generation from all eternity. They have indeed
this excuse, if any excuse can be received in
such a case, that it is impossible to find a single
text in all Scripture to prove the eternal generation of the Son. Certain, however, it is, whatever some of the moderns may allege to the
contrary, that the Son existed in the beginning,
under the name of the logos or word, and was
the first of the whole creation, by whom afterwards all other things were made both in heaven
and earth. John i. 1–3, 'in the beginning was
the Word, and the Word was with God, and
the Word was God,' etc.; xvii. 5, 'and now, O
Father, glorify me with thine own self with
the glory which I had with thee before the world
was.' Col. i. 15, 18, 'the first-born of every
creature.' Rev. iii. 14, 'the beginning of the
creation of God.' I Cor. viii. 6, 'Jesus Christ,
by whom are all things.' Eph. iii. 9, 'who
created all things by Jesus Christ.' Col. i. 16,
'all things were created by him and for him.'
Heb. i. 2, 'by whom also he made the worlds,'
whence it is said, v. 10, 'thou, Lord, in the

beginning hast laid the foundation of the earth.' [1]

All these passages prove the existence of the Son before the world was made, but they conclude nothing respecting his generation from all eternity. The other texts which are produced relate only to his metaphorical generation, that is, to his resuscitation from the dead, or to his unction to the mediatorial office, according to St. Paul's own interpretation of the second Psalm ' I will declare the decree ; Jehovah hath said unto me, Thou art my Son ; this day have I begotten thee '—which the apostle thus explains, Acts xiii. 32, 33, ' God hath fulfilled the promise unto us their children, in that he hath raised up Jesus again ; as it is also written in the second Psalm, Thou art my Son ; this day have I begotten thee.' Rom. i. 4, ' declared to be the Son of God with power, according to the spirit of holiness, by the resurrection from the dead.' Hence, Col. i. 18, Rev. i. 5, ' the first begotten of the dead.' Heb. i. 5, speaking of the exaltation of the Son above the angels ; ' for unto which of the angels said he at any time, Thou art my Son, this day have I begotten thee ? and again, I will be to him a Father, and he shall be to me a Son.' Again, v. 5, 6, with reference to the priesthood of Christ : ' so also Christ glorified not himself to be made an high priest, but he that said unto

[1] See Chapter VII, on the Creation, treatise ' On Christian Doctrine.'

him, Thou art my Son, this day have I begotten
thee : as he saith also in another place, Thou
art a priest for ever,' etc. Further, it will be
apparent from the second Psalm, that God has
begotten the Son, that is, has made him a king :
v. 6, 'yet have I set my king upon my holy
hill of Sion '; and then in the next verse, after
having anointed his King, whence the name of
Christ is derived, he says, ' this day have I begotten
thee.' Heb. i. 4, 5, 'being made so much better
than the angels, as he hath by inheritance obtained a more excellent name than they.' No
other name can be intended but that of Son, as
the following verse proves : ' for unto which of
the angels said he at any time, Thou art my
Son ; this day have I begotten thee ? ' The
Son also declares the same of himself. John x.
36, 'say ye of him whom the Father hath
sanctified, and sent into the world, Thou blasphemest, because I said, I am the Son of God ? '
By a similar figure of speech, though in a much
lower sense, the saints are also said to be begotten
of God.

It is evident however upon a careful comparison and examination of all these passages,
and particularly from the whole of the second
Psalm, that however the generation of the Son
may have taken place, it arose from no natural
necessity, as is generally contended, but was no
less owing to the decree and will of the Father

than his priesthood or kingly power, or his resuscitation from the dead. Nor is it any objection to this that he bears the title of begotten,
in whatever sense that expression is to be understood, or of God's ' own Son,' Rom. viii. 32. For
he is called the own Son of God merely because
he had no other Father besides God, whence he
himself said, that ' God was his Father,' John v. 18.
For to Adam God stood less in the relation of
Father, than of Creator, having only formed
him from the dust of the earth ; whereas he
was properly the Father of the Son made of
his own substance. Yet it does not follow from
hence that the Son is co-essential with the Father,
for then the title of Son would be least of all
applicable to him, since he who is properly the
Son is not coeval with the Father, much less of
the same numerical essence, otherwise the Father
and the Son would be one person ; nor did the
Father beget him from any natural necessity,
but of his own free will—a mode more perfect
and more agreeable to the paternal dignity ;
particularly since the Father is God, all whose
works, and consequently the works of generation,
are executed freely according to his own good
pleasure, as has been already proved from
Scripture.

For questionless, it was in God's power con-
sistently with the perfection of his own essence
not to have begotten the Son, inasmuch as

generation does not pertain to the nature of the
Deity, who stands in no need of propagation;
but whatever does not pertain to his own essence
or nature, he does not effect like a natural agent
from any physical necessity. If the generation
of the Son proceeded from a physical necessity,
the Father impaired himself by physically be-
getting a co-equal; which God could no more do
than he could deny himself; therefore the generation of the Son cannot have proceeded otherwise
than from a decree, and of the Father's own
free will.

Thus the Son was begotten of the Father in
consequence of his decree, and therefore within
the limits of time, for the decree itself must have
been anterior to the execution of the decree, as is
sufficiently clear from the insertion of the word
'to-day.' Nor can I discover on what passage
of Scripture the asserters of the eternal generation
of the Son ground their opinion, for the text in
Micah v. 2 does not speak of his generation, but
of his works, which are only said to have been
wrought 'from of old.' But this will be discussed more at large hereafter.

The Son is also called 'only begotten.' John
i. 14, 'and we beheld his glory, the glory as of
the only begotten of the Father'; v. 18, 'the
only begotten Son which is in the bosom of the
Father'; iii. 16, 18, 'he gave his only begotten
Son.' I John iv. 9, 'God sent his only begotten

Son.' Yet he is not called one with the Father
in essence, inasmuch as he was visible to sight,
and given by the Father, by whom also he was
sent, and from whom he proceeded; but he
enjoys the title of only begotten by way of
superiority, as distinguished from many others
who are also said to have been born of God. John
i. 13, 'which were born of God.' I John iii. 9,
'whosoever is born of God, doth not commit
sin.' James i. 18, 'of his own will begat he us
with the word of truth.' I John v. 1, 'whosoever believeth, etc., is born of God.' I Peter
i. 3, 'which according to his abundant mercy
hath begotten us again unto a lively hope.' But
since throughout the Scriptures the Son is never
said to be begotten, except, as above, in a metaphorical sense, it seems probable that he is called
only begotten principally because he is the one
mediator between God and man.

So also the Son is called the ' first born.' Rom.
viii. 29, 'that he might be the first born among
many brethren.' Col. i. 15, 'the first born of
every creature'; v. 18, 'the first born from
the dead.' Heb. i. 6, 'when he bringeth in the
first begotten into the world.' Rev. iii. 14, 'the
beginning of the creation of God'—all which
passages preclude the idea of his co-essentiality
with the Father, and of his generation from all
eternity. Thus it is said of Israel, Exod. iv. 22,
' thus saith Jehovah, Israel is my son, even my

first born '; and of Ephraim, Jer. xxxi. 9,
' Ephraim is my first born '; and of all the
saints, Heb. xii. 23, ' to the general assembly
of the first born.'

Hitherto only the metaphorical generation of
Christ has been considered ; but since to generate
another who had no previous existence, is to give
him being, and that if God generate by a physical
necessity, he can generate nothing but a co-equal
Deity, which would be inconsistent with self-
existence, an essential attribute of Divinity; (so
that according to the one hypothesis there would
be two infinite Gods, or according to the other
the *first* or *efficient cause* would become the *effect*,
which no man in his senses will admit); it becomes necessary to inquire how or in what sense
God the Father can have begotten the Son. This
point also will be easily explained by reference
to Scripture. For when the Son is said to be ' the
first born of every creature,' and ' the beginning of
the creation of God,' nothing can be more evident
than that God of his own will created, or generated,
or produced the Son before all things, endued with
the divine nature, as in the fulness of time he
miraculously begat him in his human nature of
the Virgin Mary. The generation of the divine
nature is described by no one with more sublimity
and copiousness than by the apostle to the
Hebrews, i. 2, 3, ' whom he hath appointed heir
of all things, by whom also he made the worlds ;

who being the brightness of his glory, and the express image of his person,' etc. It must be understood from this, that God imparted to the Son as much as he pleased of the divine nature, nay, of the divine substance itself, care being taken not to confound the substance with the whole essence, which would imply, that the Father had given to the Son what he retained numerically the same himself; which would be a contradiction of terms instead of a mode of generation. This is the whole that is revealed concerning the generation of the Son of God. Whoever wishes to be wiser than this, becomes foiled in his pursuit after wisdom, entangled in the deceitfulness of vain philosophy, or rather of sophistry, and involved in darkness.

Since, however, Christ not only bears the name of the only begotten Son of God, but is also several times called in Scripture God, notwithstanding the universal doctrine that there is but one God, it appeared to many who had no mean opinion of their own acuteness, that there was an inconsistency in this; which gave rise to an hypothesis no less strange than repugnant to reason, namely, that the Son, although personally and numerically another, was yet essentially one with the Father, and that thus the unity of God was preserved.

But unless the terms unity and duality mean the same with God as with man, it would have been to no purpose that God had so repeatedly inculcated that first commandment, that he was the one and only God, if another could be said to exist besides, who also himself ought to be believed in as the one God. Unity and duality cannot consist of one and the same essence. God is one *ens*, not two; one essence and one subsistence, which is nothing but a substantial essence. appertain to one *ens*; if two subsistences or two persons be assigned to one essence, it involves a contradiction of terms, by representing the essence as at once simple and compound. If one divine essence be common to two persons, that essence or divinity will either be in the relation of a whole to its several parts, or of a genus to its several species, or lastly of a common subject to its accidents. If none of these alternatives be conceded, there is no mode of escaping from the absurd consequences that follow, such as that one essence may be the third part of two or more.

There would have been no occasion for the supporters of these opinions to have offered such violence to reason, nay even to so much plain Scriptural evidence, if they had duly considered God's own words addressed to kings and princes, Psalm lxxxii. 6, ' I have said, Ye are gods, and all of you are children of the most High'; or those of Christ himself, John x. 35, ' if he called them gods, unto whom the word of God came,

and the Scripture cannot be broken—'; or those
of St. Paul, I Cor. viii. 5, 6, ' for though there be
that are called gods, whether in heaven or earth
(for there be gods many and lords many,) but
to us there is but one God, the Father, of whom
are all things,' etc.; or lastly of II Peter i. 4,
'that by these ye might be partakers of the
divine nature,' which implies much more than
the title of gods in the sense in which that title
is applied to kings; though no one would conclude from this expression that the saints were
co-essential with God.

Let us then discard reason in sacred matters,
and follow the doctrine of Holy Scripture exclusively. Accordingly, no one need expect that
I should here premise a long metaphysical discussion, and advocate in all its parts the drama
of the personalities in the Godhead: since it
is most evident, in the first place, from numberless
passages of Scripture, that there is in reality but
one true independent and supreme God; and as
he is called one (inasmuch as human reason and
the common language of mankind, and the Jews,
the people of God, have always considered him
as one person only, that is, one in a numerical
sense) let us have recourse to the sacred writings
in order to know who this one true and supreme
God is. This knowledge ought to be derived in
the first instance from the Gospel, since the
clearest doctrine respecting the one God must

necessarily be that copious and explanatory revelation concerning him which was delivered by Christ himself to his apostles, and by the apostles to their followers. Nor is it to be supposed that the Gospel would be ambiguous or obscure on this subject ; for it was not given for the purpose of promulgating new and incredible doctrines respecting the nature of God, hitherto utterly unheard of by his own people, but to announce salvation to the Gentiles through Messiah the Son of God, according to the promise of the God of Abraham. 'No man hath seen God at any time ; the only begotten Son, which is in the bosom of the Father, he hath declared him,' John i. 18. Let us therefore consult the Son in the first place respecting God.

According to the testimony of the Son, delivered in the clearest terms, the Father is that one true God, by whom are all things. Being asked by one of the scribes, Mark xii. 28, 29, 32, which was the first commandment of all, he answered from Deut. vi. 4, 'the first of all the commandments is, "Hear, O Israel, the Lord our God is one Lord"' ; or as it is in the Hebrew, 'Jehovah our God is one Jehovah.' The scribe assented ; 'there is one God, and there is none other one but he' ; and in the following verse Christ approves this answer. Nothing can be more clear than that it was the opinion of the scribe, as well as of the other Jews, that by the

unity of God is intended his oneness of person.
That this God was no other than God the Father,
is proved from John viii. 41, 54, ' we have one
Father, even God . . . it is my Father that
honoureth me ; of whom ye say that he is your
God '; iv. 21, ' neither in this mountain, nor
yet at Jerusalem, shall ye worship the Father.'
Christ therefore agrees with the whole people
of God, that the Father is that one and only God.
For who can believe it possible for the very first
of the commandments to have been so obscure,
and so ill-understood by the Church through
such a succession of ages, that two other persons, equally entitled to worship, should have
remained wholly unknown to the people of God,
and debarred of divine honours even to that very
day ? especially as God, where he is teaching
his own people respecting the nature of their
worship under the gospel, forewarns them that
they would have for their God the one Jehovah
whom they had always served, and David, that
is, Christ, for their King and Lord. Jer. xxx. 9,
' they shall serve Jehovah their God, and David
their King, whom I will raise up unto them.'
In this passage Christ, such as God willed that
he should be known or worshipped by his people
under the gospel, is expressly distinguished from
the one God Jehovah, both by nature and title.
Christ himself therefore, the Son of God, teaches
us nothing in the gospel respecting the one God

but what the law had before taught, and everywhere clearly asserts him to be his Father. John xvii. 3, 'this is life eternal, that they might know thee, the only true God, and Jesus Christ whom thou hast sent'; xx. 17' 'I ascend unto my Father and your Father; and to my God and your God': if therefore the Father be the God of Christ, and the same be our God, and if there be none other God but one, there can be no God beside the Father.

Paul, the apostle and interpreter of Christ, teaches the same in so clear and perspicuous a manner, that one might almost imagine the inculcation of this truth to have been his sole object. No teacher of catechumens in the Church could have spoken more plainly and expressly of the one God, according to the sense in which the universal consent of mankind has agreed to understand unity of number. I Cor. viii. 4–6, 'we know that an idol is nothing in the world, and that there is none other God but one: for though there be that are called gods, whether in heaven or in earth (as there be gods many and lords many), but to us there is but one God, the Father, of whom are all things, and we in him; and one Lord Jesus Christ, by whom are all things, and we by him.' Here the expression 'there is none other God but one,' excludes not only all other essences, but all other persons whatever; for it is expressly said in the sixth verse, 'that the

Father is that one God'; wherefore there is
no other person but one; at least in that sense
which is intended by divines, when they argue
from John xiv. 16, that there is *another*, for the
sake of asserting the personality of the Holy
Spirit. Again, to those 'who are called gods,
whether in heaven or in earth, God the Father
of whom are all things' is opposed singly; he
who is numerically 'one God,' to 'many gods.'
Though the Son be another God, yet in this passage he is called merely 'Lord'; he 'of whom
are all things' is clearly distinguished from him
'by whom are all things,' and if a difference of
causation prove a difference of essence, he is distinguished also in essence. Besides, since a numerical difference originates in difference of essence,
those who are two numerically, must be also
two essentially. There is 'one Lord,' namely, he
whom 'God the Father hath made,' Acts ii. 36,
much more therefore is the Father Lord, who
made him, though he be not here called Lord.
For he who calls the Father 'one God,' also calls
him one Lord above all, as Psalm cx. 1, 'the
Lord saith unto my Lord'—a passage which will
be more fully discussed hereafter. He who calls
Jesus Christ 'one Lord,' does not call him one
God, for this reason among others, that 'God the
Father hath made him both Lord and Christ,'
Acts ii. 36. Elsewhere therefore he calls the
Father both God and Lord of him whom he

here calls 'one Lord Jesus Christ'; Eph. i. 17,
'the God of our Lord Jesus Christ'; I Cor.
xi. 3, 'the head of Christ is God'; xv. 28, 'the
Son also himself shall be subject unto him.' If
in truth the Father be called 'the Father of Christ,'
if he be called 'the God of Christ,' if he be called
'the head of Christ,' if he be called the God to
whom Christ, described as 'the Lord,' nay, even as
'the Son himself, is subject, and shall be sub-
jected,' why should not the Father be also the
Lord of the same Lord Christ, and the God of the
same God Christ; since Christ must also be God
in the same relative manner that he is Lord
and Son? Lastly, the Father is he 'of whom,'
and 'from whom,' and 'by whom,' and 'for
whom are all things': Rom. xi. 36; Heb. ii. 10.
The Son is not he 'of whom,' but only 'by
whom'; and that not without an exception, viz.,
'all things which were made,' John i. 3, 'all
things, except him which did put all things
under him,' I Cor. xv. 27. It is evident therefore that when it is said 'all things were by
him,' it must be understood of a secondary
and delegated power; and that when the par-
ticle 'by' is used in reference to the Father,
it denotes the primary cause, as John vi. 57,
'I live by the Father'; when in reference to
the Son, the secondary and instrumental cause:
which will be explained more clearly on a future
occasion.

Again, Eph. iv. 4–6, ' there is one body and one Spirit, even as ye are called in one hope of your calling ; one Lord, one faith, one baptism ; one God and Father of all, who is above all and through all, and in you all.' Here there is one Spirit, and one Lord ; but the Father is one, and therefore God is one in the same sense as the remaining objects of which unity is predicated, that is, numerically one, and therefore one also in person.   I Tim. ii. 5, ' there is one God, and one mediator between God and men, the man Christ jesus.' Here the mediator, though not purely human, is purposely named man, by the title derived from his inferior nature, lest he should be thought equal to the Father, or the same God, the argument distinctly and expressly referring to one God. Besides, it cannot be explained how anyone can be a mediator to himself on his own behalf ; according to Gal. iii. 20, ' a mediator is not a mediator of one, but God is one.' How then can God be a mediator of God ? Not to mention that he himself uniformly testifies of himself, John viii. 28, ' I do nothing of myself,' and v. 42, ' neither came I of myself.' Undoubtedly therefore he does not act as a mediator to himself ; nor return as a mediator to himself. Rom. v. 10, ' we were reconciled to God by the death of his Son.' To whatever God we were reconciled, if he be one God, he cannot be the God by whom we are reconciled, inasmuch as that God is another person; for if he be one and the same, he must be a mediator between himself and us, and reconcile us to himself by himself; which is an insurmountable difficulty.

Though all this be so self-evident as to require no explanation—namely, that the Father alone is a self-existent God, and that a being which is not self-existent cannot be God,—it is wonderful with what futile subtleties, or rather with what juggling artifices, certain individuals have endeavoured to elude or obscure the plain meaning of these passages; leaving no stone unturned, recurring to every shift, attempting every means, as if their object were not to preach the pure and unadulterated truth of the gospel to the poor and simple, but rather by dint of vehemence and obstinacy to sustain some absurd paradox from falling, by the treacherous aid of sophisms and verbal distinctions, borrowed from the barbarous ignorance of the schools.

They defend their conduct, however, on the ground, that though these opinions may seem inconsistent with reason, they are to be received for the sake of other passages of Scripture, and that otherwise Scripture will not be consistent with itself. Setting aside reason therefore, let us have recourse again to the language of Scripture.

The passages in question are two only. The

first is John x. 30, ' I and my Father are one '—
that is, one in essence, as it is commonly interpreted. But God forbid that we should decide
rashly on any point relative to the Deity. Two
things may be called one in more than one way.
Scripture saith, and the Son saith, *I and my
Father are one*—I bow to their authority. Certain commentators conjecture that they are
one in essence—I reject what is merely man's
invention. For the Son has not left us to conjecture in what manner he is one with the Father
(whatever member of the Church may have
first arrogated to himself the merit of the dis-
covery), but explains the doctrine himself most
fully, so far as we are concerned to know it.
The Father and the Son are one, not indeed in
essence, for he had himself said the contrary
in the preceding verse, ' my Father, which gave
them me, is greater than all ' (see also xiv. 28,
' my Father is greater than I '), and in the following verses he distinctly denies that he made himself God in saying, ' I and my Father are one ' ;
he insists that he had only said as follows, which
implies far less, x. 36, ' say ye of him whom the
Father hath sanctified, and sent into the world,
Thou blasphemest ; because I said, I am the
Son of God ? ' This must be spoken of two
persons not only not co-essential, but not co-
equal. Now if the Son be laying down a doctrine
respecting the unity of the divine essence in

two persons of the Trinity, how is it that he does
not rather attribute the same unity of essence
to the three persons ?   Why does he divide the
indivisible Trinity ?   For there cannot be unity
without totality.   Therefore, on the authority
of the opinions holden by my opponents themselves, the Son and the Father without the Spirit
are not one in essence.   How then are they one ?
It is the province of Christ alone to acquaint us
with this, and accordingly he does acquaint us
with it.   In the first place, they are one, inasmuch as they speak and act with unanimity ;
and so he explains himself in the same chapter,
after the Jews had misunderstood his saying :
x. 38, ' believe the works ; that ye may know and
believe that the Father is in me, and I in him ' ;
xiv. 10, ' believest thou not that I am in the
Father, and the Father in me ? the words that
I speak unto you, I speak not of myself, but the
Father that dwelleth in me, he doeth the works.'
Here he evidently distinguishes the Father from
himself in his whole capacity, but asserts at the
same time that the Father remains in him ;
which does not denote unity of essence, but only
intimacy of communion.   Secondly, he declares
himself to be one with the Father in the same
manner as we are one with him—that is, not
in essence, but in love, in communion, in agreement, in charity, in spirit, in glory.   John xiv.
20, 21, ' at that day ye shall know that I am

in the Father, and ye in me, and I in you : he that hath my commandments, and keepeth them, he it is that loveth me ; and he that loveth me, shall be loved of my Father '; xvii. 21, ' that they all may be one, as thou, Father, art in me, and I in thee ; that they also may be one in us '; v. 23, ' I in them, and thou in me, that they may be made perfect in one, and that the world may know that thou hast sent me, and hast loved them as thou hast loved me '; v. 22, ' the glory which thou gavest me I have given them, that they may be one, even as we are one.' When the Son has shown in so many modes how he and the Father are one, why should I set them all aside ? why should I, on the strength of my own reasoning, though in opposition to reason itself, devise another mode, which makes them one in essence ; or why, if already devised by some other person, adopt it, in preference to Christ's own mode ? If it be proposed on the single authority of the Church, the true doctrine of the orthodox Church herself teaches me other-wise ; inasmuch as it instructs me to listen to the words of Christ before all other.

The other passage, and which according to the general opinion affords the clearest founda-tion for the received doctrine of the essential unity of the three persons, is I John v. 7, ' there are three that bear record in heaven, the Father, the Word, and the Holy Ghost, and these three

are one.' But not to mention that this verse
is wanting in the Syriac and the other two Oriental
versions, the Arabic and the Ethiopic, as well
as in the greater part of the ancient Greek manuscripts, and that in those manuscripts which
actually contain it many various readings occur,
it no more necessarily proves those to be essentially one, who are said to be one in heaven,
than it proves those to be essentially one, who
are said in the following verse to be one on earth.
And not only Erasmus, but even Beza, however
unwillingly, acknowledged (as may be seen in
their own writings) that if John be really the
author of the verse, he is only speaking here,
as in the last quoted passage, of an unity of
agreement and testimony. Besides, who are the
three who are said to bear witness ? That they
are three Gods will not be admitted ; therefore
neither is it the one God, but one record or one
testimony of three witnesses, which is implied.
But he who is not co-essential with God the
Father, cannot be co-equal with the Father.
This text, however, will be discussed more at large
in the following chapter.

But, it is objected, although Scripture does not
say in express words that the Father and Son
are one in essence, yet reason proves the truth
of the doctrine from the texts quoted above, as
well as from other passages of Scripture.

In the first place, granting (which I am far

from doing) that this is the case, yet on a subject so sublime, and so far above our reason, where the very elements and first postulates, as it were, of our faith are concerned, belief must be founded, not on mere reason, but on the Word of God exclusively, where the language of the revelation is most clear and particular. Reason itself, however, protests strongly against the doctrine in question; for how can reason establish (as it must in the present case) a position contrary to reason? Undoubtedly the product of reason must be something consistent with reason, not a notion as absurd as it is removed from all human comprehension. Hence we conclude, that this opinion is agreeable neither to Scripture nor reason. The other alternative therefore must be adopted, namely, that if God be one God, and that one God be the Father, and if notwithstanding the Son be also called God, the Son must have received the name and nature of Deity from God the Father, in conformity with his decree and will, after the manner stated before. This doctrine is not disproved by reason, and Scripture teaches it in innumerable passages.

But those who insist that the Son is one God with the Father, consider their point as susceptible of ample proof, even without the two texts already examined (on which indeed some admit that no reliance is to be placed), if it can be demonstrated from a sufficient number of Scripture testimonies that the name, attributes, and works of God, as well as divine honours, are habitually ascribed to the Son. To proceed therefore in the same line of argument, I do not ask them to believe that the Father alone and none else is God, unless I shall have proved, first, that in every passage each of the particulars above mentioned is attributed in express terms only to one God the Father, as well by the Son himself as by his apostles. Secondly, that wherever they are attributed to the Son, it is in such a manner that they are easily understood to be attributable in their original and proper sense to the Father alone; and that the Son acknowledges himself to possess whatever share of Deity is assigned to him by virtue of the peculiar gift and kindness of the Father; as the apostles also testify. And lastly, that the Son himself and his apostles acknowledge throughout the whole of their discourses and writings, that the Father is greater than the Son in all things.

I am aware of the answer which will be here made by those who, while they believe in the unity of God, yet maintain that the Father alone is not God. I shall therefore meet their objection in the outset, lest they should raise a difficulty and outcry at each individual passage. They twice beg the question, or rather require us to make two gratuitous concessions. In the

first place, they insist, that wherever the name
of God is attributed to the Father alone, it should
be understood οὐσιωδῶς, not ὑποστατικῶς, that is to
say, that the name of the Father, who is unity,
should be understood to signify the three persons,
or the whole essence of the Trinity, not the
single person of the Father. This is on many
accounts a ridiculous distinction and invented
solely for the purpose of supporting their peculiar
opinion ; although in reality, instead of supporting
it, it will be found to be dependent on it, and
therefore if the opinion itself be invalidated, for
which purpose a simple denial is sufficient, the
futile distinction falls to the ground at the same
time. For the fact is, not merely that the distinction is a futile one, but that it is no distinction
at all ; it is a mere verbal quibble, founded on the
use of synonymous words, and cunningly dressed
up in terms borrowed from the Greek to dazzle the
eyes of novices. For since *essence* and *hypostasis*
mean the same thing,[1] it follows that there can be
no real difference of meaning between the adverbs
essentially and *substantially* [*hypostatice*], which
are derived from them. If then the name
of God be attributed to the Father alone
essentially, it must also be attributed to the
Father alone *substantially* ; since one substantial
essence means nothing else than one hypostasis,
and *vice versa*. I would therefore ask my

---

[1] See Chapter II of the treatise ' On Christian Doctrine.'

adversaries, whether they hold the Father to be an abstract *ens* or not? Questionless they will reply, the primary *ens* of all. I answer, therefore, that as he has one hypostasis, so must he have one essence proper to himself, incommunicable in the highest degree, and participated by no one, that is, by no person besides, for he cannot have his own proper hypostasis, without having his own proper essence. For it is impossible for any *ens* to retain its own essence in common with any other thing whatever, since by this essence it is what it is, and is numerically distinguished from all others. If therefore the Son, who has his own proper hypostasis, have not also his own proper essence, but the essence of the Father, he becomes on their hypothesis either no *ens* at all, or the same *ens* with the Father; which strikes at the very foundation of the Christian religion. The answer which is commonly made, is ridiculous—namely, that although one finite essence can pertain to one person only, one infinite essence may pertain to a plurality of persons; whereas in reality the infinitude of the essence affords an additional reason why it can pertain to only one person. All acknowledge that both the essence and the person of the Father are infinite; therefore the essence of the Father cannot be communicated to another person, for otherwise there might be two, or any imaginable number of infinite persons.

The second postulate is, that wherever the
Son attributes Deity to the Father alone, and
as to one greater than himself, he must be understood to speak in his human character, or as
mediator. Wherever the context and the fact
itself require this interpretation, I shall readily
concede it, without losing anything by the concession; for however strongly it may be contended, that when the Son attributes everything
to the Father alone, he speaks in his human or
mediatorial capacity, it can never be inferred
from hence that he is one God with the Father.
On the other hand, I shall not scruple to deny
the proposition, whenever it is to be conceded
not to the sense of the passage, but merely to
serve their own theory; and shall prove that
what the Son attributes to the Father, he attributes in his filial or even in his divine character
to the Father as God of God, and not to himself
under any title or pretence whatever.

With regard to the name of God, wherever
simultaneous mention is made of the Father
and the Son, that name is uniformly ascribed to
the Father alone, except in such passages as shall
be hereafter separately considered. I shall quote
in the first place the texts of the former class,
which are by far the more considerable in point
of number, and form a large and compact body
of proofs. John iii. 16, ' God so loved the world,
that he gave his own Son,' etc.; vi. 27, ' him

hath God the Father sealed'; v. 29, 'this is
the work of God, that ye believe on him whom
he hath sent'; xiv. 1, 'ye believe in God, believe
also in me.' What is meant by believing in any
one, will be explained hereafter; in the mean-
time it is clear that two distinct things are here
intended—'in God' and 'in me.' Thus all the
apostles in conjunction, Acts iv. 24-26, 'lifted
up their voice to God with one accord, and said,
Lord, thou art God which hast made heaven and
earth . . . who by the mouth of thy servant
David hast said, Why did the heathen rage . . .
against the Lord, and against his Christ?' Rom.
viii. 3, 'God sending his own Son.' I Thess. iii.
11, 'now God himself, and our Father, and our
Lord Jesus Christ, direct our way unto you.'
Col. ii. 2, 'to the acknowledgment of the mystery
of God, and of the Father, and of Christ'; iii. 3,
'your life is hid with Christ in God.' II Tim.
iv. 1, 'I charge thee therefore before God and
the Lord Jesus Christ.' I John iv. 9, 'the love
of God toward us, because that God sent his only
begotten Son.' So also where Christ is named
first in order. Gal. i. 1, 'by Jesus Christ, and
God the Father, who raised him from the dead.'
II Thess. ii. 16, 'now our Lord Jesus Christ
himself, and God, even our Father.' The same
thing may be observed in the very outset of all
the Epistles of St. Paul and of the other apostles,
where, as is natural, it is their custom to declare

in express and distinct terms who he is by whose
divine authority they have been sent. Rom.
i. 7, 8; I Cor. i. 1–3; II Cor. i. 1–3; and so
throughout to the book of Revelation. See
also Mark i. 1.

The Son likewise teaches that the attributes
of divinity belong to the Father alone, to the
exclusion even of himself. With regard to
omniscience. Matt. xxiv. 36, 'of that day and
hour knoweth no man, no not the angels of heaven,
but my Father only'; and still more explicitly,
Mark xiii. 32, 'not the angels which are in heaven,
neither the Son, but the Father.'

With regard to supreme dominion both in
heaven and earth, the unlimited authority and
full power of decreeing according to his own
independent will. Matt. vi. 13, 'thine is the
kingdom and the power and the glory for ever';
xviii. 35, 'so likewise shall my heavenly Father
do also unto you, if ye from your hearts forgive
not,' etc.; xxvi. 29, 'in my Father's kingdom';
xx. 23, 'to sit on my right hand and on my left,
is not mine to give, but it shall be given to them
for whom it is prepared of my Father.' It 'is
not mine'—in my mediatorial capacity, as it is
commonly interpreted. But questionless when the
ambition of the mother and her two sons incited
them to prefer this important demand, they
addressed their petition to the entire nature of
Christ, how exalted soever it might be, praying

him to grant their request to the utmost extent of his power whether as God or man ; v. 20, 'worshipping him, and desiring a certain thing of him,' and v. 21, 'grant that they may sit.' Christ also answers with reference to his whole nature—' it is not mine to give ' ; and lest for some reason they might still believe the gift belonged to him, he declares that it was altogether out of his province, and the exclusive privilege of the Father. If his reply was meant solely to refer to his mediatorial capacity, it would have bordered on sophistry, which God forbid that we should attribute to him ; as if he were capable of evading the request of Salome and her sons by the quibble which the logicians call *expositio prava* or *æquivoca*, when the respondent answers in a sense or with a mental intention different from the meaning of the questioner. The same must be said of other passages of the same kind, where Christ speaks of himself ; for after the hypostatical union of two natures in one person, it follows that whatever Christ says of himself, he says not as the possessor of either nature separately, but with reference to the whole of his character, and in his entire person, except where he himself makes a distinction. Those who divide this hypostatical union at their own discretion, strip the discourses and answers of Christ of all their sincerity ; they represent everything as ambiguous and uncertain, as true and false at the same time; it is not Christ that speaks, but some unknown substitute, sometimes one, and sometimes another; so that the words of Horace may be justly applied to such disputants :—

Quo teneam vultus mutantem Protea nodo ?

Luke xxiii. 34, 'Father, forgive them,' etc. John xiv. 2, 'in my Father's house.' So also Christ himself says, Matt. xxvi. 39, 'O my Father, if it be possible, let this cup pass from me; nevertheless not as I will, but as thou wilt.' Now it is manifest that those who have not the same will, cannot have the same essence. It appears, however, from many passages, that the Father and Son have not, in a numerical sense, the same intelligence or will. Matt. xxiv. 36, 'no man knoweth . . . but my Father only.' Mark xiii. 32, 'neither the Son, but the Father.' John vi. 38, 'I came down from heaven, not to do mine own will, but the will of him that sent me.' Those therefore whose understanding and will are not numerically the same, cannot have the same essence. Nor is there any mode of evading this conclusion, inasmuch as this is the language of the Son himself respecting his own divine nature. See also Matt. xxvi. 42, and v. 53, 'thinkest thou that I cannot now pray to my Father, and he shall presently give me more than twelve legions of angels ? ' Mark xiv. 36, 'Abba, Father, all things are possible unto thee; take away this cup from

me,' etc.   Luke xxii. 29, 'I appoint unto you a
kingdom, as my Father hath appointed unto me';
xxiii. 46, 'Father, into thy hands I commend my
spirit.'   John xii. 27, 'Father, save me from this
hour.'   If these prayers be uttered only in his
human capacity, which is the common explanation, why does he petition these things from
the Father alone instead of from himself, if he
were God?   Or rather, supposing him to be at
once man and the supreme God, why does he ask
at all for what was in his own power?   What
need was there for the union of the divine and
the human nature in one person, if he himself,
being equal to the Father, gave back again into
his hands everything that he had received
from him?

With regard to his supreme goodness.   Matt.
xix. 17, 'why callest thou me good?   there is
none good but one, that is, God.'   We need not
be surprised that Christ should refuse to accept
the adulatory titles which were wont to be given
to the Pharisees, and on this account should
receive the young man with less kindness than
usual; but when he says, 'there is none good but
one, that is, God,' it is evident that he did not
choose to be considered essentially the same
with that one God; for otherwise this would
only have been disclaiming the credit of goodness
in one character, for the purpose of assuming
it in another.   John vi. 32, 'my Father giveth

you the true bread from heaven'; v. 65, 'no man can come unto me'—that is, to me, both God and man—'except it were given unto him of my Father.'

With regard to his supreme glory. Matt. xviii. 10, 'their angels do always behold the face of my Father which is in heaven.' John xvii. 4, 'I have glorified thee on the earth.' Nay, it is to those who obey the Father that the promise of true wisdom is made even with regard to the knowing Christ himself, which is the very point now in question. John vii. 17, 18, 'if any man will do his will, he shall know of the doctrine whether it be of God, or whether I speak of myself: he that speaketh of himself speaketh of his own glory; but he that seeketh his glory that sent him, the same is true, and no unrighteousness is in him'; xv. 8, 'herein is my Father glorified, that ye bear much fruit; so shall ye be my disciples.' Matt. vii. 21, 'not every one that saith unto me, Lord, Lord, shall enter into the kingdom of heaven, but he that doeth the will of my Father that is in heaven'; xii. 50, 'whosoever shall do the will of my Father which is in heaven, the same is my brother, and sister, and mother.'

Thus Christ assigns every attribute of the Deity to the Father alone. The apostles uniformly speak in a similar manner. Rom. xv. 5, 6, 'the God of patience and consolation grant you

to be like-minded one toward another, according
to Christ Jesus'; xvi. 25–27, 'to him that is
of power to stablish you . . . according to the
commandment of the everlasting God . . . to
God only wise, be glory through Jesus Christ—
our Lord,' as the Vetus Interpres and some of
the Greek manuscripts read it.   I Tim. vi. 13–16,
'I give thee charge in the sight of God, who
quickeneth all things, and before Christ Jesus,
who witnessed a good confession . . . until the
appearing of our Lord Jesus Christ, which in his
times he shall shew, who is the blessed and only
Potentate, the King of kings, and Lord of lords;
who alone hath immortality, dwelling in the
light which no man can approach unto, whom
no man hath seen, nor can see; to whom be
honour and power everlasting.   Amen.'

With regard to his works.   See Rom. xvi. 25–
27; I Tim. vi. 13–16, as quoted above.   II Cor.
i. 21, 22, 'now he which stablisheth us with
you in Christ, and hath anointed us, is God;
who hath also sealed us.'   Now the God which
stablisheth us, is one God.   I Peter i. 2, 'elect
according to the foreknowledge of God the Father,
through sanctification of the Spirit unto obedience and sprinkling of the blood of Jesus Christ.'
Even those works which regard the Son himself,
or which were done in him.   Acts v. 30–33, 'the
God of our fathers raised up Jesus . . . him
hath God exalted with his right hand to be a

Prince and a Saviour, for to give repentance to Israel, and forgiveness of sins.' Gal. i. 1, 'by Jesus Christ, and God the Father, who raised him from the dead.' Rom. x. 9, 'if thou shalt believe in thine heart that God hath raised him from the dead, thou shalt be saved.' I Cor. vi. 14' 'God hath both raised up the Lord, and will also raise us up by his own power.' I Thess. i. 10, 'to wait for his Son from heaven, whom he raised from the dead.' Heb. x. 5, 'sacrifice and offering thou wouldest not, but a body hast thou prepared me.' I Peter i. 21, 'who by him do believe in God that raised him up from the dead.' So many are the texts wherein the Son is said to be raised up by the Father alone, which ought to have greater weight than the single passage in St. John ii. 19, 'destroy the temple, and in three days I will raise it up '—where he spake briefly and enigmatically, without explaining his meaning to enemies who were unworthy of a fuller answer, on which account he thought it unnecessary to mention the power of the Father.

With regard to divine honours. For as the Son uniformly pays worship and reverence to the Father alone, so he teaches us to follow the same practice. Matt. vi. 6, 'pray to thy Father'; v. 9, 'after this manner therefore pray ye: Our Father, which art in heaven,' etc.; xviii. 19, 'as touching any thing that they shall ask, it shall be done for them of my Father which is in heaven.' Luke xi. 1, 2, 'teach us to pray,' etc., 'and he said unto them, When ye pray, say, Our Father which art in heaven' John ii. 16, 'make not my Father's house an house of merchandise'; iv. 21-23, 'the hour cometh and now is, when the true worshippers shall worship the Father in spirit and in truth; for the Father seeketh such to worship him'; xv. 16, 'that whatsoever ye shall ask of the Father in my name, he may give it you'; xvi. 23, 'in that day ye shall ask me nothing; . . . whatsoever ye shall ask the Father in my name, he will give it you.' Rom. i. 8, 9, 'first, I thank my God through Jesus Christ for you all . . . for God is my witness, whom I serve with my spirit in the gospel of his Son,' etc.; v. 11, 'we also joy in God through our Lord Jesus Christ'; vii. 25, 'I thank God through Jesus Christ our Lord'; xv. 6, 'that ye may with one mind and one mouth glorify God, even the Father of our Lord Jesus Christ.' I Cor. i. 4, 'I thank my God always on your behalf, for the grace of God which is given you by Jesus Christ'; II Cor. i. 3, 'blessed be God, even the Father of our Lord Jesus Christ, the Father of mercies, and the God of all comfort.' Gal. i. 4, 5, 'who gave himself   according to the will of God and our Father; to whom be glory for ever and ever.' Eph. i. 3, 'blessed be the God and Father of our Lord Jesus Christ,' etc.; ii. 18, 'for through him we both have

access by one Spirit unto the Father'; iii. 14,
' for this cause I bow my knees unto the Father
of our Lord Jesus Christ.' v. 20, 21, 'now unto
him that is able to do exceeding abundantly
above all that we ask or think, according to the
power that worketh in us, unto him be glory in
the church by Christ Jesus, throughout all ages,
world without end.' Philippians i. 2, 3, ' grace
be unto you and peace from God our Father,
and from the Lord Jesus Christ. I thank my God
upon every remembrance of you.' See also Col.
i. 3, and iii. 17, ' whatsoever ye do . . . do all
in the name of the Lord Jesus, giving thanks
to God and the Father by him.' I Thess. i. 2, 3,
' we give thanks to God for you all, making
mention of you in our prayers : remembering
without ceasing your work of faith, and labour
of love, and patience of hope in our Lord Jesus
Christ, in the sight of God and our Father';
v. 9, 10, ' to serve the living and true God ; and
to wait for his Son from heaven, whom he raised
from the dead.' See also II Thess. i. 2, 3, and II
Tim. i. 3, ' I thank God, whom I serve from my
forefathers.' Now the forefathers of Paul served
God the Father alone. See also Philem. 4, 5,
and I Peter i. 3 and iv. 10, 11, ' as every man
hath received the gift . . . let him speak as the
oracles of God . . . as of the ability which
God giveth, that God in all things may be glorified
through Jesus Christ.' James i. 27, ' pure re-

ligion and undefiled before God and the Father,
is this.' I John ii. 1, ' we have an advocate with
the Father, Jesus Christ the righteous'; II John
4-6, ' walking in truth, as we have received a
commandment from the Father   this is love,
that we walk after his commandments.' Rev.
i. 6, ' who made us kings and priests unto God
and his Father ; to him be glory and dominion
for ever and ever.' Matt. xxi. 12, ' Jesus went
into the temple of God.' Here however my
opponents quote the passage from Malachi iii. 1,
' the Lord whom ye seek shall suddenly come to
his temple, even the messenger of the covenant.'
I answer, that in prophetical language these
words signify the coming of the Lord into the
flesh, or into the temple of the body, as it is
expressed John ii. 21. For the Jews sought no
one in the temple as an object of worship, except
the Father ; and Christ himself in the same
chapter has called the temple his Father's house,
and not his own. Nor were they seeking God,
but ' that Lord and messenger of the covenant ';
that is, him who was sent from God as the mediator
of the covenant ;—he it was who should come to
his Church, which the prophets generally express
figuratively under the image of the temple. So
also where the terms God and man are put in
opposition to each other, the Father stands
exclusively for the one God. James iii. 9, ' there-
with bless we God, even the Father ; and there-

.with curse we men, which are made after the similitude of God.' I John ii. 15, 16, ' if any man love the world, the love of the Father is not in him : for all that is in the world . . . is not of the Father, but of the world.'

But it is strenuously urged on the other hand, that the Son is sometimes called God, and even Jehovah ; and that all the attributes of the Deity are assigned to him likewise in many passages both of the Old and New Testament. We arrive therefore at the other point which I originally undertook to prove ; and since it has been already shown from the analogy of Scripture, that where the Father and the Son are mentioned together, the name, attributes, and works of the Deity, as well as divine honours, are always assigned to the one and only God the Father, I will now demonstrate, that whenever the same properties are assigned to the Son, it is in such a manner as to make it easily intelligible that they ought all primarily and properly to be attributed to the Father alone.

It must be observed in the first place, that the name of God is not unfrequently ascribed, by the will and concession of God the Father, even to angels and men,—how much more then to the only begotten Son, the image of the Father. To angels. Psalm xcvii. 7, 9, ' worship him all ye gods . . . thou art high above all the earth ; thou art exalted far above all gods,' compared

with Heb. i. 6.   See also Psalm viii. 5.   To judges.
Exod. xxii. 28, ' thou shalt not revile the gods,
nor curse the ruler of thy people.'   See also, in
the Hebrew, Exod. xxi. 6, xxii. 8, 9 ; Psalm
lxxxii. 1, 6, ' he judgeth among the gods.'   ' I
have said, Ye are gods, and all of you are children
of the most High.'   To the whole house of David,
or to all the Saints.   Zech. xii. 8, ' the house of
David shall be as God, as the angel of the Lord
before them.'   The word אֱלֹהִים, though it be
of the plural number, is also employed to signify
a single angel, in case it should be thought that
the use of the plural implies a plurality of persons in the Godhead : Judges xiii. 21, ' then
Manoah knew that he was an angel of Jehovah :
and Manoah said unto his wife, We shall surely
die, because we have seen God.'   The same
word is also applied to a single false god.   Exod.
xx. 3, ' thou shalt have no other gods before me.'
To Dagon : Judges xvi. 23.   To single idols
I Kings xi. 33.   To Moses : Exod. iv. 16 and
vii. 1.   To God the Father alone : Psalm ii. 7,
xlv. 7, and in many other places.   Similar to
this is the use of the word אֲדֹנִים, *the Lord*, in
the plural number with a singular meaning ;
and with a plural affix according to the Hebrew
mode.   The word אֲדֹנָי also with the vowel
Patha is frequently employed to signify one man,
and with the vowel *Kamets* to signify one God,
or one angel bearing the character of God.   This

peculiarity in the above words has been carefully noticed by the grammarians and lexicographers themselves, as well as in בַּעַל used appellatively. The same thing may perhaps be remarked of the proper names בְּעָלִים and עֲשְׁתָּרוֹת· For even among the Greeks, the word δεσπότης, that is, Lord, is also used in the plural number in the sense of the singular, when extraordinary respect and honour are intended to be paid. Thus in the Iphigenia in Aulis of Euripides, λίαν δεσπόταισι πιστὸς εἶ [l. 304, Beck's edition] for δεσπότῃ, and again εὐκλεὲς τοι δεσποτῶν θνῄσκειν ὑπερ [l. 312] for δεσπότου. It is also used in the Rhesus and the Bacchæ in the same manner.

Attention must be paid to these circumstances, lest anyone through ignorance of the language should erroneously suppose, that whenever the word Elohim is joined with a singular, it is intended to intimate a plurality of persons in unity of essence. But if there be any significance at all in this peculiarity, the word must imply as many gods as it does persons. Besides, a plural adjective or a plural verb is sometimes joined to the word Elohim, which, if a construction of this kind could mean anything, would signify not a plurality of persons only, but also of natures. See in the Hebrew, Deut. v. 26 ; Josh. xxiv. 19 ; Jer. x. 10 ; Gen. xx. 13. Further, the singular אֱלֹהַּ also sometimes occurs, Deut. xxxii. 18, and elsewhere. And the singular noun אָדוֹן is

joined with Jehovah, Exod. xxiii. 17. It is also
attributed to Christ with the singular affix, Psalm
cx. 1, לַאדֹנִי 'Jehovah said unto my Lord,' in
which passage the Psalmist speaks of Christ (to
whom the name of *Lord* is assigned, as a title of
the highest honour) both as distinct from Jehovah,
and, if any reliance can be placed on the affix, as
inferior to Jehovah. But when he addresses the
Father, the affix is changed, and he says, v. 5,
אֲדֹנָי 'the Lord at thy right hand shall strike
through kings in the day of his wrath.'

The name of God seems to be attributed to
angels because as heavenly messengers they bear
the appearance of the divine glory and person,
and even speak in the very words of the Deity.
Gen. xxi. 17, 18, xxii. 11, 12, 15, 16, ' by myself
have I sworn, saith Jehovah.' For the expression so frequently in the mouth of the prophets,
and which is elsewhere often omitted, is here
inserted, for the purpose of shewing that angels
and messengers do not declare their own words,
but the commands of God who sends them, even
though the speaker seem to bear the name and
character of the Deity himself. So believed the
patriarch Jacob: Gen. xxxi. 11–13, ' the angel
of God spake unto me, saying . . . I have seen
all that Laban doeth unto thee. I am the God of
Bethel,' etc.; xxxii. 30, ' I have seen God face
to face'; compared with Hos. xii. 3, 4, ' he
had power with God, yea, he had power over the

angel.' Exod. xxiv. 10, 11, 'they saw the God
of Israel . . . also they saw God.' Deut. iv.
33, ' did ever people hear the voice of God speaking out of the midst of the fire, as thou hast heard,
and live ? ' Yet it is said, Exod. xxxiii. 20,
' there shall no man see me, and live.' John
i. 18, ' no man hath seen God at any time '; v.
37, ' ye have neither heard his voice at any time,
nor seen his shape.' I Tim. vi. 16, ' dwelling in
the light which no man can approach unto,
whom no man hath seen, nor can see.' It follows therefore that whoever was heard or seen, it
was not God ; not even where mention is made
of God, nay, even of Jehovah himself, and of
the angels in the same sentence. Gen. xxvⅢ.
12, 13, ' behold the angels of God . . . and
behold, Jehovah stood above them.' I Kings
xxii. 19, ' I saw Jehovah sitting on his throne,
and all the host of heaven standing by him '
Isa. vi. 1, 2, ' I saw the Lord sitting upon a
throne . . . above it stood the seraphim.' I
repeat, it was not God himself that he saw, but
perhaps one of the angels clothed in some modifi-
cation of the divine glory, or the Son of God
himself, the image of the glory of his Father,
as John understands the vision, xii. 41, ' these
things said Esaias, when he saw his glory.' For
if he had been of the same essence, he could no
more have been seen or heard than the Father
himself, as will be more fully shewn hereafter.

Hence even the holiest of men were troubled in mind when they had seen an angel, as if they had seen God himself. Gen. xxxii. 30, ' I have seen God.' Judges vi. 22, ' when Gideon perceived that he was an angel of Jehovah, Gideon said, Alas, O Lord Jehovah, for because I have seen an angel of Jehovah face to face.' See also xiii. 21, 22, as before.

The name of God is ascribed to judges, because they occupy the place of God to a certain degree in the administration of judgment. The Son, who was entitled to the name of God both in the capacity of a messenger and of a judge, and indeed in virtue of a much better right, did not think it foreign to his character, when the Jews accused him of blasphemy because he made himself God, to allege in his own defence the very reason which has been advanced. John x. 34–36, ' Jesus answered them, Is it not written in your law, I said, Ye are gods ? If he called them gods unto whom the word of God came, and the Scripture cannot be broken ; say ye of him whom the Father hath sanctified and sent into the world, Thou blasphemest ; because I said, I am the Son of God ? '—especially when God himself had called the judges children of the Most High, as has been stated before. Hence I Cor. viii. 5, 6, ' for though there be that are called gods, whether in heaven or in earth, (as there be gods many, and lords many,) but to us there is but one God, the Father, of whom are all things, and we in him ; and one Lord Jesus Christ, by whom are all things, and we by him.'

Even the principal texts themselves which are brought forward to prove the divinity of the Son, if carefully weighed and considered, are sufficient to shew that the Son is God in the manner which has been explained. John i. 1, ' in the beginning was the Word, and the Word was with God, and the Word was God.' It is not said, from everlasting, but ' in the beginning.' ' The Word ' —therefore the Word was audible. But God, as he cannot be seen, so neither can he be heard ; John v. 37. The Word therefore is not of the same essence with God. ' The Word was with God, and was God '—namely, because he was with God, that is, in the bosom of the Father, as it is expressed, v. 18. Does it follow therefore that he is one in essence with him with whom he was ? It no more follows, than that the disciple 'who was lying on Jesus' breast,' John xiii. 23, was one in essence with Christ. Reason rejects the doctrine ; Scripture nowhere asserts it ; let us therefore abandon human devices, and follow the evangelist himself, who is his own interpreter. Rev. xix. 13, ' his name is called the Word of God '—that is, of the one God : he himself is a distinct person. If therefore he be a distinct person, he is distinct from God, who is unity. How then is he himself also God ? By the same right as he enjoys the title of the Word, or of the only begotten Son, namely, by the will of the one God. This seems to be the reason why it is repeated in the second verse—'the same was in the beginning with God'; which enforces what the apostle wished we should principally observe, not that he was in the beginning God, but in the beginning with God; that he might show him to be God only by proximity and love, not in essence; which doctrine is consistent with the subsequent explanations of the evangelist in numberless passages of his gospel.

Another passage is the speech of Thomas, John xx. 28, 'My Lord and my God.' He must have an immoderate share of credulity who attempts to elicit a new confession of faith, unknown to the rest of the disciples, from this abrupt exclamation of the apostle, who invokes in his surprise not only Christ his own Lord, but the God of his ancestors, namely, God the Father; as if he had said, Lord! what do I see— what do I hear—what do I handle with my hands? He whom Thomas is supposed to call God in this passage, had acknowledged respecting himself not long before, v. 17, 'I ascend unto my God and your God.' Now the God of God cannot be essentially one with him whose God he is. On whose word therefore can we ground our faith with most security; on that of Christ, whose doctrine is clear, or of Thomas, a new disciple, first incredulous, then suddenly breaking out into an abrupt exclamation in an ecstasy of wonder, if indeed he really called Christ his God? For having reached out his fingers, he called the man whom he touched, as if unconscious of what he was saying, by the name of God. Neither is it credible that he should have so quickly understood the hypostatic union of that person whose resurrection he had just before disbelieved. Accordingly the faith of Peter is commended ' blessed art thou, Simon '—for having only said—' thou art the Son of the living God,' Matt. xvi. 16, 17. The faith of Thomas, although as it is commonly explained, it asserts the divinity of Christ in a much more remarkable manner, is so far from being praised, that it is undervalued, and almost reproved in John xx. 29, ' Thomas, because thou hast seen me, thou hast believed; blessed are they that have not seen, and yet have believed.' And yet, though the slowness of his belief may have deserved blame, the testimony borne by him to Christ as God, which, if the common interpretation be received as true, is clearer than occurs in any other passage, would undoubtedly have met with some commendation; whereas it obtains none whatever. Hence there is nothing to invalidate that interpretation of the passage which has been already suggested, referring the words—' my Lord '—to Christ—' my God '—to God the

E

Father, who had just testified that Christ was his Son, by raising him up from the dead in so wonderful a manner.

So too Heb. i. 8, 'unto the Son'—or 'of the Son' —' he saith, Thy throne, O God, is for ever and ever.' But in the next verse it follows, 'thou hast loved righteousness,' etc., 'therefore God, even thy God, hath anointed thee with the oil of gladness above thy fellows,' where almost every word indicates the sense in which Christ is here termed God; and the words of Jehovah put into the mouth of the bridal virgins, Psalm xlv., might have been more properly quoted by this writer for any other purpose than to prove that the Son is co-equal with the Father, since they are originally applied to Solomon, to whom, as appropriately as to Christ, the title of God might have been given on account of his kingly power, conformably to the language of Scripture.

. These three passages are the most distinct of all that are brought forward; for the text in Matt. i. 23, 'they shall call' (for so the great majority of the Greek manuscripts read it) 'his name Immanuel, which being interpreted is, God with us,' does not prove that he whom they were so to call should necessarily be God, but only a messenger from God, according to the song of Zacharias, Luke i. 68, 69, 'blessed be the Lord God of Israel; for he hath visited and redeemed his people, and hath raised up an horn of salvation for us,' etc. Nor can anything certain be inferred from Acts xvi. 31, 34, 'believe on the Lord Jesus Christ—and he rejoiced, believing in God with all his house.' For it does not follow from hence that Christ is God, since the apostles have never distinctly pointed out Christ as the ultimate object of faith ; but these are merely the words of the historian, expressing briefly what the apostles doubtless inculcated in a more detailed manner—faith in God the Father through Christ. Nor is the passage in Acts xx. 28 more decisive—' the Church of God, which he hath purchased with his own blood'; that is, with his own Son, as it is elsewhere expressed, for God properly speaking has no blood ; and no usage is more common than the substitution of the figurative term blood for offspring. But the Syriac version reads, not ' the Church of God,' but ' the Church of Christ '; and in our own recent translation it is, ' the Church of the Lord.' Nor can any certain dependence be placed on the authority of the Greek manuscripts, five of which read τοῦ Κυρίου καὶ Θεοῦ, according to Beza, who suspects that the words τοῦ Κυρίου have crept in from the margin, though it is more natural to suppose the words καὶ Θεοῦ to have crept in, on account of their being an addition to the former. The same must be said respecting Rom. ix. 5, ' who is over all, God blessed for ever. Amen.' For in the first place, Hilary

and Cyprian do not read the word *God* in this
passage, nor do some of the other Fathers, if we
may believe the authority of Erasmus ; who has
also shewn that the difference of punctuation
may raise a doubt with regard to the true meaning of the passage, namely, whether the clause
in question should not rather be understood of
the Father than of the Son.   But waiving these
objections, and supposing that the words are
spoken of the Son ; they have nothing to do
with his essence, but only intimate that divine
honour is communicated to the Son by the
Father, and particularly that he is called God ;
which is nothing more than what has been already fully shown by other arguments.   But, it is
said, the same words which were spoken of the
Father, Rom. i. 25, ' the Creator, who is blessed
for ever.   Amen,' are here repeated of the Son ;
therefore the Son is equal to the Father.   If
there be any force in this reasoning, it will rather
prove that the Son is greater than the Father ;
for according to the ninth chapter, he is ' over
all,' which, however, they remind us, ought to be
understood in the same sense as John iii. 31, 32,
' he that cometh from above, is above all ; he that
cometh from heaven is above all.'   In these words
even the divine nature is clearly implied, and yet,
' what he hath seen and heard, that he testifieth,'
which language affirms that he came not of himself, but was sent from the Father, and was

obedient to him. It will be answered, that it
is only his mediatorial character which is intended.
But he never could have become a mediator,
nor could he have been sent from God, or have
been obedient to him, unless he had been inferior
to God and the Father as to his nature. Therefore also after he shall have laid aside his functions
as mediator, whatever may be his greatness, or
whatever it may previously have been, he must
be subject to God and the Father. Hence he
is to be accounted above all, with this reserva-
tion, that he is always to be excepted ' who did
put all things under him,' I Cor. xv. 27, and
who consequently is above him under whom
he has put all things. If lastly he be termed
' blessed,' it must be observed that he received
blessing as well as divine honour, not only as
God, but even as man. Rev. v. 12, ' worthy is
the Lamb that was slain to receive power, and
riches, and wisdom, and strength, and honour,
and glory, and blessing '; and hence, v. 13,
' blessing, and honour, and glory, and power, be
unto him that sitteth upon the throne, and unto
the Lamb for ever and ever.'

There is a still greater doubt respecting the
reading in I Tim. iii. 16, ' God was manifest in
the flesh.' Here again Erasmus asserts that
neither Ambrose nor the Vetus Interpres reads
the word God in this verse, and that it does not
appear in a considerable number of the early

copies. However this may be, it will be clear,
when the context is duly examined, that the
whole passage must be understood of God the
Father in conjunction with the Son. For it is
not Christ who is ' the great mystery of godliness,'
but God the Father in Christ, as appears from
Col. ii. 2, ' the mystery of God and of the Father,
and of Christ.' II Cor. v. 18, 19, ' all things
are of God, who hath reconciled us to himself
by Jesus Christ . . . to wit, that God was in
Christ, reconciling the world unto himself, not
imputing their trespasses unto them.' Why
therefore should God the Father not be in Christ
through the medium of all those offices of reconciliation which the apostle enumerates in
this passage of Timothy ? ' God was manifest in
the flesh '—namely, in the Son, his own image ;
in any other way he is invisible : nor did Christ
come to manifest himself, but his Father, John
xiv. 8, 9. ' Justified in the Spirit '—and who
should be thereby justified, if not the Father ?
' Seen of angels '—inasmuch as they desired to
look into this mystery. I Peter i. 12, ' preached
unto the Gentiles '—that is, the Father in Christ.
' Believed on in the world '—and to whom is
faith so applicable, as to the Father through
Christ ? ' Received up into glory '—namely, he
who was in the Son from the beginning, after
reconciliation had been made, returned with the
Son into glory, or was received into that supreme

glory which he had obtained in the Son. But there is no need of discussing this text at greater length : those who are determined to defend at all events the received opinion, according to which these several propositions are predicated not of the Father but of the Son alone, when they are in fact applicable both to the one and the other, though on different grounds, may easily establish that the Son is God, a truth which I am far from denying—but they will in vain attempt to prove from this passage that he is the supreme God, and one with the Father.

The next passage is Titus ii. 13, ' the glorious appearing of the great God and our Saviour Jesus Christ.' Here also the glory of God the Father may be intended, with which Christ is to be invested on his second advent, Matt. xvi. 27, as Ambrose understands the passage from the analogy of Scripture. For the whole force of the proof depends upon the definitive article, which may be inserted or omitted before the two nouns in the Greek without affecting the sense ; or the article prefixed to one may be common to both. Besides, in other languages, where the article is not used, the words may be understood to apply indifferently either to one or two persons ; and nearly the same words are employed without the article in reference to two persons, Philipp. i. 2, and Philem. 3, except that in the latter passages the word ' Father ' is substituted for 'great.' So also II Peter i. 1, 'through the righteousness of [our] God and our Saviour Jesus Christ.' Here the repetition of the pronoun ἡμῶν without the article, as it is read by some of the Greek manuscripts, shews that two distinct persons are spoken of. And surely what is proposed to us as an object of belief, especially in a matter involving a primary article of faith, ought not to be an inference forced and extorted from passages relating to an entirely different subject, in which the readings are sometimes various, and the sense doubtful—nor hunted out by careful research from among articles and particles—nor elicited by dint of ingenuity, like the answers of an oracle, from sentences of dark or equivocal meaning—but should be susceptible of abundant proof from the clearest sources. For it is in this that the superiority of the gospel to the law consists; this, and this alone, is consistent with its open simplicity; this is that true light and perspicuity which we had been taught to expect would be its characteristic. Lastly, he who calls God, 'great,' does not necessarily call him supreme, or essentially one with the Father; nor on the other hand does he thereby deny that Christ is 'the great God,' in the sense in which he has been above proved to be such.

Another passage which is also produced is I John iii. 16, 'hereby perceive we the love of

God, because he laid down his life for us.' Here, however, the Syriac version reads *illius* instead of *Dei*, and it remains to be seen whether other manuscripts do the same. The pronoun *he*, ἐκεῖνος seems not to be referred to God, but to the Son of God, as may be concluded from a comparison of the former chapters of this epistle, and the first, second, fifth, and eighth verses of the chapter before us, as well as from Rom. v. 8, ' God commendeth his love toward us, in that, while we were yet sinners, Christ died for us.' ' The love of God,' therefore, is the love of the Father, whereby he so loved the world, that ' he purchased it with his own blood,' Acts xx. 28, and for it ' laid down his life,' that is, the life of his only begotten Son, as it may be explained from John iii. 16, and by analogy from many other passages. Nor is it extraordinary that by the phrase, ' his life,' should be understood the life of his beloved Son, since we are ourselves in the habit of calling any much-loved friend by the title of life, or part of our life, as a term of endearment in familiar discourse.

But the passage which is considered most important of all, is I John v. part of the twentieth verse— for if the whole be taken, it will not prove what it is adduced to support. ' We know that the Son of God is come, and hath given us an understanding, that we may know him that is true, and we are in him that is true, (even) in his

Son Jesus Christ : this is the true God, and eternal
life.' For 'we are in him that is true, in his Son'
—that is, so far as we are in the Son of him that
is true :—' this is the true God ' ; namely, he who
was just before called 'him that was true,' the
word *God* being omitted in the one clause, and
subjoined in the other. For he it is that
is 'he that is true' (whom that we might
know, 'we know that the Son of God is
come, and hath given us an understanding ')
not he who is called 'the Son of him that
is true,' though that be the nearest antecedent
—for common sense itself requires that the article
' this ' should be referred to 'him that is true '
(to whom the subject of the context principally
relates), not to ' the Son of him that is true.' Ex-
amples of a similar construction are not wanting.
See Acts iv. 10, 11, and x. 16 ; II Thess. ii. 8, 9 ;
II John 7. Compare also John xvii. 3, with which
passage the verse in question seems to correspond
exactly in sense, the position of the words alone
being changed. But it will be objected, that
according to some of the texts quoted before,
Christ is God ; now if the Father be the only
true God, Christ is not the true God ; but if he
be not the true God, he must be a false God. I
answer, that the conclusion is too hastily drawn ;
for it may be that he is not 'he that is true,' either
because he is only the image of him that is true,
or because he uniformly declares himself to be

inferior to him that is true. We are not obliged
to say of Christ what the Scriptures do not say.
The Scriptures call him ' God,' but not ' him that is
the true God ' ; why are we not at liberty to acqui-
esce in the same distinction ? At all events *he*
is not to be called a false God, to whom, as to
his beloved Son, he that is the true God has
communicated his divine power and glory.

They also adduce Phil. ii. 6, ' who being in the
form of God.' But this no more proves him to
be God than the phrase which follows—' took
upon him the form of a servant '—proves that
he was really a servant, as the sacred writers
nowhere use the word ' form ' for actual being.
But if it be contended that ' the form of God ' is
here taken in a philosophical sense for the essential form, this consequence cannot be avoided,
that when Christ laid aside the form, he laid aside
also the substance and the efficiency of God ;
a doctrine against which they protest, and with
justice ' To be in the form of God,' therefore,
seems to be synonymous with being in the image
of God; which is often predicated of Christ, even
as man is also said, though in a much lower sense,
to be the image of God, that is, by creation. More
will be added respecting this passage hereafter.

The last passage that is quoted is from the
epistle of Jude 4, ' denying the only Lord God,
and our Lord Jesus Christ.' Who will not agree
that this is too verbose a mode of description,

if all these words are intended to apply to one person ? or who would not rather conclude, on a comparison of many other passages which tend to confirm the same opinion, that they were spoken of two persons, namely, the Father the only God, and our Lord Jesus Christ ? Those, however, who are accustomed to discover some extraordinary force in the use of the article, contend that both names must refer to the same person, because the article is prefixed in the Greek to the first of them only, which is done to avoid weakening the structure of the sentence. If the force of the articles is so great, I do not see how other languages can dispense with them.

The passages quoted in the New Testament from the Old will have still less weight than the above, if produced to prove anything more than what the writer who quoted them intended. Of this class are, Psalm lxviii. 17–19, ' the chariots of God are twenty thousand, etc. . . . the Lord is among them, etc. . . . thou hast ascended on high . thou hast received gifts for men.' Here (to say nothing of several ellipses, which the interpreters are bold enough to fill up in various ways, as they think proper) mention is made of two persons, ' God ' and ' the Lord,' which is in contradiction to the opinions of those who attempt to elicit a testimony to the supreme divinity of Christ, by comparing this passage with Eph. iv. 5–8. Such a doctrine was never intended by the apostle, who argues very differently in the ninth verse—' now that he ascended, what is it but that he also descended first into the lower parts of the earth ? '—from which he only meant to show that the Lord Christ, who had lately died, and was now received into heaven, ' gave gifts unto men ' which he had received from the Father.

It is singular, however, that those who maintain the Father and the Son to be one in essence, should revert from the gospel to the times of the law, as if they would make a fruitless attempt to illustrate light by darkness. They say that the Son is not only called God, but also Jehovah, as appears from a comparison of several passages in both testaments. Now Jehovah is the one supreme God ; therefore the Son and the Father are one in essence. It will be easy, however, to expose the weakness of an argument derived from the ascription of the name of Jehovah to the Son. For the name of Jehovah is conceded even to the angels, in the same sense as it has been already shewn that the name of God is applied to them, namely, when they represent the divine presence and person, and utter the very words of Jehovah. Gen. xvi. 7, ' the angel of Jehovah found her,' compared with v. 10, ' the angel of Jehovah said unto her, I will multiply thy seed exceedingly,' and v. 13, ' she called the name of Jehovah who spake unto her—.' xviii. 13,

' and Jehovah said,' etc., whereas it appears
that the three men whom Abraham entertained
were angels. Gen. xix. 1, ' there came two
angels'; v. 13, ' and Jehovah hath sent us '—
compared with v. 18, 21, 24, ' Oh, not so, אֲדֹנָי
and he said unto him, See, I have accepted thee
. then Jehovah rained . . . from Jehovah out
of heaven.' Gen. xxi. 17, ' the angel of God
called to Hagar out of heaven . . . God hath
heard' compared with v. 18, 'I will make
him a great nation.' So Exod. iii. 2, 4, ' the
angel of Jehovah . . . when Jehovah saw that
he turned aside to see, God called unto him '—
compared with Acts vii. 30, ' there appeared to
him an angel of the Lord in a flame of fire in a
bush.' If that angel had been Christ or the
supreme God, it is natural to suppose that Stephen
would have declared it openly, especially on such
an occasion, where it might have tended to
strengthen, the faith of the other believers, and
strike his judges with alarm. In Exod. xx., on
the delivery of the law to Moses, no mention is
made of anyone, except Jehovah, and yet Acts
vii. 38 the same Stephen says, ' this is he that was
in the church in the wilderness with the angel
which spake to him in the mount Sina '; and v.
53 he declares that ' the law was received by
the disposition of angels.' Gal. iii. 19, ' it was
ordained by angels.' Heb. ii. 2, ' if the word
spoken by angels was steadfast,' etc. Therefore

what is said in Exodus to have been spoken by
Jehovah, was not spoken by himself personally,
but by angels in the name of Jehovah. Nor is
this extraordinary, for it would seem unsuitable
that Christ the minister of the gospel should
also have been the minister of the law: 'by
how much more also he is the mediator of a
better covenant,' Heb. viii. 6. On the other
hand it would indeed have been wonderful if
Christ had actually appeared as the mediator
of the law, and none of the apostles had ever
intimated it. Nay, the contrary seems to be
asserted, Heb. i. 1, 2, 'God who at sundry times
and in divers manners spake in times past unto
the fathers by the prophets, hath in these last
days spoken unto us by his Son.' Again it is
said, Num. xxii. 22, 'God's anger was kindled
       and the angel of Jehovah stood in the way
for an adversary unto him'; v. 31, 'then
Jehovah opened the eyes of Balaam, and he
saw the angel of Jehovah.' Afterward the same
angel speaks as if he were Jehovah himself, v. 32,
'behold I went out to withstand thee, because
thy way is perverse before me': and Balaam
says, v. 34, 'if it displease thee—'; to which
the angel answers—'only the word that I shall
speak unto thee, that thou shalt speak.' v. 35
compared with v. 20 and with chap. xxiii. 8, 20.
Josh. v. 14, 'as captain of the host of Jehovah
am I come,' compared with vi. 2, 'Jehovah

said unto Joshua.' Judges vi. 11, 12, 'an angel
of Jehovah   the angel of Jehovah'—compared with v. 14, 'Jehovah looked upon him,
and said—.' Again, v. 20, 21, 'the angel of God
. . . the angel of Jehovah'; and v. 22, 'Gideon
perceived that he was an angel of Jehovah'—
compared with v. 23, 'Jehovah said unto him'
—although the angel here, as in other instances,
personated the character of Jehovah :—v. 14,
'have not I sent thee ?'; v. 16, 'surely I will be
with thee, and thou shalt smite the Midianites':
and Gideon himself addresses him as Jehovah,
v. 17, 'show me a sign that thou talkest with
me.' I Chron. xxi. 15, 'God sent an angel—';
v. 16, 17, 'and David saw the angel of Jehovah
. . . and fell upon his face, and said unto God—';
v. 18, 19, 'then the angel of Jehovah commanded
Gad to say unto David . . . and David went up
at the saying of Gad, which he spake in the name
of Jehovah.'

But it may be urged, that the name of Jehovah
is sometimes assigned to two persons in the same
sentence. Gen. xix. 24, 'Jehovah rained . . .
from Jehovah out of heaven.' I Sam. iii. 21,
'Jehovah revealed himself unto Samuel in Shiloh
by the word of Jehovah.' Jer. xxxiv. 12, 'the
word of Jehovah came to Jeremiah from Jehovah,
saying—.' Hos. i. 7, 'I will save them by Jehovah their God.' Zech. iii. 1–3, 'standing
before the angel . . . and Jehovah said unto

Satan, Jehovah rebuke thee'—and again, 'before the angel.' I answer, that in these passages either one of the two persons is an angel, according to that usage of the word which has been already explained ; or it is to be considered as a peculiar form of speaking, in which, for the sake of emphasis, the name of Jehovah is repeated, though with reference to the same person : 'for Jehovah the God of Israel is one Jehovah.' If in such texts as these both persons are to be understood properly and in their own nature as Jehovah, there is no longer one Jehovah, but two ; whence it follows that the repetition of the name can only have been employed for the purpose of giving additional force to the sentence. A similar form of speech occurs, Gen. ix. 16, 'I will look upon it, that I may remember the everlasting covenant between God and every living creature'; and I Cor. i. 7, 'waiting for the coming of our Lord Jesus Christ.' I Thess. iii. 12, 13, 'the Lord make you to increase, etc., to the end he may stablish your hearts . before God, even our Father, at the coming of our Lord Jesus Christ.' Here whether it be 'God, even our Father,' or 'our Lord Jesus,' who is in the former verse called 'Lord,' in either case there is the same redundance. If the Jews had understood the passages quoted above, and others of the same kind, as implying that there were two persons, both of whom were Jehovah, and both of whom had an equal right to the appellation, there can be no doubt that, seeing the doctrine so frequently enforced by the prophets, they would have adopted the same belief which now prevails among us, or would at least have laboured under considerable scruples on the subject: whereas I suppose no one in his senses will venture to affirm that the Jewish Church ever so understood the passages in question, or believed that there were two persons, each of whom was Jehovah, and had an equal right to assume the title. It would seem, therefore, that they interpreted them in the manner above mentioned. Thus in allusion to a human being, I Kings viii. 1, 'then Solomon assembled the elders of Israel . . . unto king Solomon in Jerusalem.' No one is so absurd as to suppose that the name of Solomon is here applied to two persons in the same sentence. It is evident, therefore, both from the declaration of the sacred writer himself, and from the belief of those very persons to whom the angels appeared, that the name of Jehovah was attributed to an angel; and not to an angel only, but also to the whole church, Jer. xxxiii. 16.

But as Placæus of Saumur thinks it incredible that an angel should bear the name of Jehovah, and that the dignity of the supreme Deity should be degraded by being personated, as it were on a stage, I will produce a passage in which God himself declares that his name is in an angel.

Exod. xxiii. 20, 21, 'behold, I send an angel before thee, to keep thee in the way, etc., beware of him, and obey his voice; provoke him not, for he will not pardon your transgressions; for my name is in him.' The angel who from that time forward addressed the Israelites, and whose voice they were commanded to hear, was always called Jehovah, though the appellation did not properly belong to him. To this they reply, that he was really Jehovah, for that angel was Christ; I Cor. x. 9, 'neither let us tempt Christ,' etc. I answer that it is of no importance to the present question, whether it were Christ or not; the subject of inquiry now is, whether the children of Israel understood that angel to be really Jehovah? If they did so understand, it follows that they must have conceived either that there were two Jehovahs, or that Jehovah and the angel were one in essence; which no rational person will affirm to have been their belief. But even if such an assertion were advanced, it would be refuted by Exod. xxxiii. 2, 3, 5, 'I will send an angel before thee . . . for I will not go up in the midst of thee . . . lest I consume thee in the way. And when the people heard these evil tidings, they mourned.' If the people had believed that Jehovah and that angel were one in essence, equal in divinity and glory, why did they mourn, and desire that Jehovah should go up before them, notwithstanding his anger,

rather than the angel? who, if he had indeed
been Christ, would have acted as a mediator and
peace-maker. If, on the contrary, they did not
consider the angel as Jehovah, they must necessarily have understood that he bore the name
of Jehovah in the sense in which I suppose him
to have borne it, wherein there is nothing either
absurd or histrionic. Being at length prevailed
upon to go up with them in person, he grants
thus much only, v. 14, 'my presence shall go with
thee'—which can imply nothing else than a
representation of his name and glory in the
person of some angel. But whoever this was,
whether Christ, or some angel different from the
preceding, the very words of Jehovah himself
show that he was neither one with Jehovah, nor
co-equal, for the Israelites are commanded to
hear his voice, not on the authority of his own
name, but because the name of Jehovah was in
him. If on the other hand it is contended that
the angel was Christ, this proves no more than
that Christ was an angel, according to their
interpretation of Gen. xlviii. 16, 'the angel
which redeemed me from all evil'; and Isa. lxiii.
9, 'the angel of his presence saved them'—that
is, he who represented his presence or glory,
and bore his character; an angel, or messenger,
as they say, by office, but Jehovah by nature.
But to whose satisfaction will they be able to
prove this? He is called indeed, Mal. iii. 1,

'the messenger of the covenant': see also
Exod. xxiii. 20, 21, compared with I Cor. x. 9,
as before.   But it does not therefore follow, that
whenever an angel is sent from heaven, that
angel is to be considered as Christ ; nor where
Christ is sent, that he is to be considered as one
God with the Father. Nor ought the obscurity
of the law and the prophets to be brought forward to refute the light of the gospel, but on the
contrary the light of the gospel ought to be
employed to illustrate the obscurity necessarily
arising from the figurative language of the
prophets. However this may be, Moses says,
prophesying of Christ, Deut. xviii. 15, ' Jehovah
thy God will raise up unto thee a prophet from
the midst of thee, of thy brethren, like unto me ;
unto him ye shall hearken.'   It will be answered
that he here predicts the human nature of Christ.
I reply that in the following verse he plainly
takes away from Christ that divine nature which
it is wished to make co-essential with the Father,
' according to all that thou desiredst of Jehovah
thy God in Horeb . . . saying, Let me not hear
again the voice of Jehovah my God,' etc.   In
hearing Christ, therefore, as Moses himself predicts and testifies, they were not to hear the God
Jehovah, nor were they to consider Christ as
Jehovah.
  . The style of the prophetical book of Revelation, as respects this subject, must be regarded

in the same light. Chap. i. 1, 8, 11, 'he sent and signified it by his angel.' Afterwards this angel (who is described nearly in the same words as the angel, Dan. x. 5, etc.) says, 'I am Alpha and Omega, the beginning and the ending, saith the Lord, which is, and which was, and which is to come'; v. 13, 'like unto the Son of man'; v. 17, 'I am the first and the last'; ii. 7, etc., 'what the Spirit saith unto the churches'; xxii. 6, 'the Lord God sent his angel'; v. 8, 'before the feet of the angel which showed me these things'; v. 9, 'see thou do it not; for I am thy fellow-servant,' etc. Again, the same angel says, v. 12, '.behold, I come quickly, and my reward is with me,' etc., and again, v. 13, 'I am Alpha and Omega,' etc., and v. 14, 'blessed are they that do his commandments,' and v. 16, 'I Jesus have sent my angel,' etc. These passages so perplexed Beza, that he was compelled to reconcile the imaginary difficulty by supposing that the order of a few verses in the last chapter had been confused and transposed by some Arian (which he attributed to the circumstance of the book having been acknowledged as canonical by the Church at a comparatively late period, and therefore less carefully preserved), whence he thought it necessary to restore them to what he considered their proper order. This supposition would have been unnecessary, had he remarked, what may be uniformly observed throughout the Old Testament, that angels are accustomed to assume the name and person, and the very words of God and Jehovah, as their own ; and that occasionally an angel represents the person and the very words of God, without taking the name either of Jehovah or God, but only in the character of an angel, or even of a man, as Junius himself acknowledges, Judges ii. 1, etc. But according to divines the name of Jehovah signifies two things, either the nature of God, or the completion of his word and promises. If it signify the nature, and therefore the person of God, why should not he who is invested with his person and presence, be also invested with the name which represents them ? If it signify the completion of his word and promises, why should not he, to whom words suitable to God alone are so frequently attributed, be permitted also to assume the name of Jehovah, whereby the completion of these words and promises is represented ? Or if that name be so acceptable to God, that he has always chosen to consider it as sacred and peculiar to himself alone, why has he uniformly disused it in the New Testament, which contains the most important fulfilment of his prophecies ; retaining only the name of the Lord, which had always been common to him with angels and men ? If, lastly, any name whatever can be so pleasing to God, why has he exhibited himself to us in the gospel without any proper name at all ?

They urge, however, that Christ himself is sometimes called Jehovah in his own name and person ; as in Isa. viii. 13, 14, ' sanctify Jehovah of hosts himself, and let him be your fear, and let him be your dread : and he shall be for a sanctuary ; but for a stone of stumbling and for a rock of offence to both the houses of Israel,' etc., compared with I Peter ii. 7, 8, ' the same is made the head of the corner, and a stone of stumbling,' etc.   I answer, that it appears on a comparison of the thirteenth with the eleventh verse—' for Jehovah spake thus to me,' etc.—that these are not the words of Christ exhorting the Israelites to sanctify and fear himself, whom they had not yet known, but of the Father threatening, as in other places, that he would be ' for a stone of stumbling, etc., to both the houses of Israel,' that is, to the Israelites, and especially to the Israelites of that age.   But supposing the words to refer to Christ, it is not unusual among the prophets for God the Father to declare that he would work himself, what afterwards under the gospel he wrought by means of his Son.   Hence Peter says—' the same is˙ made the head of the corner, and a stone of stumbling.'   By whom made, except by the Father ?   And in the third chapter, a quotation of part of the same passage of Isaiah clearly proves that the Father was speaking of himself ; v. 15, ' but sanctify the

Lord God '—under which name no one will assert
that Christ is intended. Again, they quote Zech.
xi. 13, ' Jehovah said unto me, Cast it unto the
potter ; a goodly price that I was prized at of
them ' That this relates to Christ I do not
deny ; only it must be remembered, that this
is not his own name, but that the name of Jehovah
was in him, Exod. xxiii. 21, as will presently
appear more plainly. At the same time there is
no reason why the words should not be understood of the Father speaking in his own name,
who would consider the offences which the Jews
should commit against his Son, as offences against
himself ; in the same sense as the Son declares
that whatever is done to those who believed in
him, is done to himself. Matt. xxv. 35, 40, ' I
was an hungred, and ye gave me meat, etc.,
inasmuch as ye have done it unto one of the least
of these my brethren, ye have done it unto me.'
An instance of the same kind occurs, Acts ix.
4, ' Saul, Saul, why persecutest thou me ? ' The
same answer must be given respecting Zech.
xii. 10, especially on a comparison with Rev.
i. 7, ' every eye shall see him, and they also that
pierced him '; for none have seen Jehovah at
any time, much less have they seen him as a man ;
least of all have they pierced him. Secondly, they
pierced him who ' poured upon them the spirit
of grace,' Zech. xii. 10. Now it was the Father
who poured the spirit of grace through the Son ;

Acts ii. 33, 'having received of the Father the promise of the Holy Ghost, he hath shed forth this.' Therefore it was the Father whom they pierced in the Son. Accordingly, John does not say, 'they shall look upon me,' but, 'they shall look upon him whom they pierced,' chap. xix. 37. So also in the verse of Zechariah alluded to, a change of persons takes place—'they shall look upon me whom they have pierced, and they shall mourn for him as one mourneth for his only son'; as if Jehovah were not properly alluding to himself, but spoke of another, that is, of the Son. The passage in Malachi iii. 1, admits of a similar interpretation : 'behold I will send my messenger, and he shall prepare the way before me, and Jehovah, whom ye seek, shall suddenly come to his temple, even the messenger of the covenant, whom ye delight in : behold he shall come, saith Jehovah of hosts.' From which passage Placæus argues thus : He before whose face the Baptist is to be sent as a messenger, is the God of Israel ; but the Baptist was not sent before the face of the Father ; therefore Christ is that God of Israel. But if the name of Elias could be ascribed to John the Baptist, Matt. xi. 14, inasmuch as he 'went before him in the spirit and power of Elias,' Luke i. 17, why may not the Father be said to send him before his own face, inasmuch as he sends him before the face of him who was to come in

the name of the Father? for that it was the
Father who sent the messenger, is proved by the
subsequent words of the same verse, since the
phrases 'I who sent,' and 'the messenger of the
covenant who shall come,' and 'Jehovah of
hosts who saith these things,' can scarcely be
understood to apply all to the same person. Nay,
even according to Christ's own interpretation, the
verse implies that it was the Father who sent
the messenger; Matt. xi. 10, 'behold, I send my
messenger before thy face.' Who was it that
sent?—the Son, according to Placæus. Before
the face of whom?—of the Son: therefore the
Son addresses himself in this passage, and sends
himself before his own face, which is a new and
unheard of figure of speech; not to mention
that the Baptist himself testifies that he was
sent by the Father, John i. 33, 'I knew him not,
but he that sent me . . . the same said unto
me,' etc. God the Father therefore sent the
messenger before the face of his Son, inasmuch
as that messenger preceded the advent of the
Son; he sent him before his own face, inasmuch
as he was himself in Christ, or, which is the same
thing, in the Son, 'reconciling the world unto
himself,' II Cor. v. 19. That the name and
presence of God is used to imply his vicarious
power and might resident in the Son, is proved
by another prophecy concerning John the Baptist,
Isa. xl. 3, 'the voice of him that crieth in the

wilderness, Prepare ye the way of Jehovah;
make straight in the desert a highway for our
God.' For the Baptist was never heard to cry
that Christ was *Jehovah* or *our God.*

Recurring, however, to the Gospel itself, on
which, as on a foundation, our dependence should
chiefly be placed, and adducing my proofs more
especially from the evangelist John, the leading
purpose of whose work was to declare explicitly
the nature of the Son's divinity, I proceed to
demonstrate the other proposition announced in
my original division of the subject—namely, that
the Son himself professes to have received from
the Father, not only the name of God and of
Jehovah, but all that pertains to his own being—
that is to say, his individuality, his existence itself,
his attributes, his works, his divine honours; to
which doctrine the apostles also, subsequent to
Christ, bear their testimony. John iii. 35, ' the
Father loveth the Son, and hath given all things
unto him,'; xiii. 3, ' Jesus knowing that the
Father had given all things unto him, and that
he was come from God.' Matt. xi. 27, ' all things
are delivered unto me of my Father.'

But here perhaps the advocates of the contrary
opinion will interpose with the same argument
which was advanced before; for they are con-
stantly shifting the form of their reasoning,
Vertumnus-like, and using the twofold nature of
Christ developed in his office of mediator, as a

ready subterfuge by which to evade any arguments that may be brought against them. What Scripture says of the Son generally, they apply, as suits their purpose, in a partial and restricted sense; at one time to the Son of God, at another to the Son of Man—now to the Mediator in his divine, now in his human capacity, and now again in his union of both natures. But the Son himself says expressly, 'the Father loveth the Son, and hath given all things into his hand,' John iii. 35—namely, because 'he loveth him,' not because he hath begotten him—and he hath given all things to him as 'the Son,' not as Mediator only. If the words had been meant to convey the sense attributed to them by my opponents, it would have been more satisfactory and intelligible to have said, *the Father loveth Christ*, or *the Mediator*, or *the Son of Man*. None of these modes of expression are adopted, but it is simply said, 'the Father loveth the Son'; that is, whatever is comprehended under the name of the Son. The same question may also be repeated which was asked before, whether from the time that he became the Mediator, his Deity, in their opinion, remained what it had previously been, or not? If it remained the same, why does he ask and receive everything from the Father, and not from himself? If all things come from the Father, why is it necessary (as they maintain it to be) for the mediatorial office, that he should be the true and supreme God; since he has received from the Father whatever belongs to him, not only in his mediatorial, but in his filial character? If his Deity be not the same as before, he was never the supreme God. From hence may be understood John xvi. 15, 'all things that the Father hath are mine'—that is, by the Father's gift. And xvii. 9, 10, 'them which thou hast given me, for they are thine; and all mine are thine, and thine are mine.'

In the first place, then, it is most evident that he receives his name from the Father. Isa. ix. 6, 'his name shall be called Wonderful, etc., the everlasting Father'; if indeed this elliptical passage be rightly understood: for, strictly speaking, the Son is not the Father, and cannot properly bear the name, nor is it elsewhere ascribed to him, even if we should allow that in some sense or other it is applied to him in the passage before us. The last clause, however, is generally translated not 'the everlasting Father,' but 'the Father of the age to come'—that is, its teacher, the name of father being often attributed to a teacher. Philipp. ii. 9, 'wherefore God also hath highly exalted him, and hath given him (καὶ ἐχαρίσατο) a name which is above every name.' Heb. i. 4, 'being made so much better than the angels, as he hath by inheritance obtained a more excellent name than they.' Eph. i. 20, 21, 'when he set him at his own right hand far above all principality, etc., and every name that is named, not only in this world, but also in that which is to come.' There is no reason why that name should not be Jehovah, or any other name pertaining to the Deity, if there be any still higher : but the imposition of a name is allowed to be uniformly the privilege of the greater personage, whether father or lord.

We need be under no concern, however, respecting the name, seeing that the Son receives his very being in like manner from the Father. John vii. 29, ' I am from him.' The same thing is implied John i. 1, ' in the beginning.' For the notion of his eternity is here excluded not only by the decree, as has been stated before, but by the name of Son, and by the phrases—' this day have I begotten thee,' and ' I will be to him a father.' Besides, the word ' beginning ' can only here mean ' before the foundation of the world,' according to John xvii. 5, as is evident from Col. i. 15–17, ' the first born of every creature : for by him were all things created that are in heaven, and that are in earth, etc., and he is before all things, and by him all things consist.' Here the Son, not in his human or mediatorial character, but in his capacity of creator, is himself called the first born of every creature. So too Heb. ii. 11, ' for both he that sanctifieth, and they that are sanctified, are all of one '; and iii. 2, ' faithful

to him that appointed him.' Him who was
begotten from all eternity the Father cannot have
begotten, for what was made from all eternity
was never in the act of being made; him whom
the Father begat from all eternity he still begets;
he whom he still begets is not yet begotten, and
therefore is not yet a Son; for an action which
has no beginning can have no completion. Besides, it seems to be altogether impossible that the
Son should be either begotten or born from all
eternity. If he is the Son, either he must have
been originally in the Father, and have proceeded
from him, or he must always have been as he is
now, separate from the Father, self-existent and
independent. If he was originally in the Father,
but now exists separately, he has undergone a
certain change at some time or other, and is
therefore mutable. If he always existed separately from, and independently of, the Father,
how is he from the Father, how begotten, how
the Son, how separate in subsistence, unless
he be also separate in essence? since (laying
aside metaphysical trifling) a substantial essence
and a subsistence are the same thing. However
this may be, it will be universally acknowledged
that the Son now at least differs numerically
from the Father; but that those who differ
numerically must differ also in their proper
essences, as the logicians express it, is too clear
to be denied by anyone possessed of common

reason. Hence it follows that the Father and the Son differ in essence.

That this is the true doctrine, reason shews on every view of the subject ; that it is contrary to Scripture, which my opponents persist in maintaining, remains to be proved by those who make the assertion. Nor does the type of Melchisedec, on which so much reliance is placed, involve any difficulty. Heb. vii. 3, 'without father, without mother, without descent ; having neither beginning of days, nor end of life ; but made like unto the Son of God.' For inasmuch as the Son was without any earthly father, he is in one sense said to have had no beginning of days ; but it no more appears that he had no beginning of days from all eternity, than that he had no Father, or was not a Son. If, however, he derived his essence from the Father, let it be shown how that essence can have been supremely divine, that is, identically the same with the essence of the Father ; since the divine essence, whose property it is to be always one, cannot possibly generate the same essence by which it is generated, nor can a subsistence or person become an agent or patient under either of the circumstances supposed, unless the entire essence be simultaneously agent or patient in the same manner also. Now as the effect of generation is to produce something which shall exist independently of the generator, it follows that God

G

cannot beget a co-equal Deity, because unity
and infinity are two of his essential attributes.
Since therefore the Son derives his essence from
the Father, he is posterior to the Father not
merely in rank [*ordine*] (a distinction unauthorized
by Scripture, and by which many are deceived),
but also in essence; and the filial character itself,
on the strength of which they are chiefly wont to
build his claim to supreme divinity, affords the
best refutation of their opinion.   For the supreme
God is self-existent;   but he who is not self-
existent, who did not beget, but was begotten,
is not the first cause, but the effect, and therefore
is not the supreme God.   He who was begotten
from all eternity, must have been from all eternity;
but if he can have been begotten who was from
all eternity, there is no reason why the Father
himself should not have been begotten, and have
derived his origin also from some paternal essence.
Besides, since father and son are relative terms,
distinguished from each other both in theory and
in fact, and since according to the laws of con-
traries the father cannot be the son, nor the
son the father, if (which is impossible from the
nature of relation) they were of one essence, it
would follow that the father stood in a filial
relation to the son, and the son in a paternal
relation to the father,—a position, of the extrava-
gance of which any rational being may judge.
For the doctrine which holds that a plurality of

hypostasis is consistent with a unity of essence, has already been sufficiently confuted. Lastly, if the Son be of the same essence with the Father, and the same Son after his hypostatical union coalesce in one person with man, I do not see how to evade the inference, that man also is the same person with the Father, an hypothesis which would give birth to not a few paradoxes. But more may perhaps be said on this point, when the incarnation of Christ comes under consideration.

With regard to his existence. John v. 26, 'as the Father hath life in himself, so hath he given to the Son to have life in himself'; vi. 57, 'as the living Father hath sent me, and I live by the Father, so he that eateth me,' etc. This gift of life is for ever. Heb. i. 8, 'unto the Son he saith, Thy throne, O God, is for ever and ever,'—hence v. 11, 12, 'they shall perish, but thou remainest . . . but thou art the same, and thy years shall not fail.'

With regard to the divine attributes. And first, that of Omnipresence; for if the Father has given all things to the Son, even his very being and life, he has also given him to be wherever he is. In this sense is to be understood John i. 48, 'before that Philip called thee . . . I saw thee.' For Nathanael inferred nothing more from this than what he professes in the next verse—'thou art the Son of God,' and iii. 13, 'the Son of man which is in heaven.' These words can

never prove that the Son, whether of man or of
God, is of the same essence with the Father;
but only that the Son of man came down from
heaven at the period of his conception in the
womb of the Virgin, that though he was minister-
ing on earth in the body, his whole spirit and mind,
as befitted a great prophet, were in the Father,—
or that he, who when made man was endowed
with the highest degree of virtue, by reason of
that virtue, or of a superior nature given to him in
the beginning, is even now 'in heaven'; or rather
'which was in heaven,' the Greek ὤν having both
significations. Again, Matt. xviii. 20, 'there am
I in the midst of them'; xxviii. 20, 'I am with
you alway, even unto the end of the world.'
Even these texts, however, do not amount to an
assertion of absolute omnipresence, as will be
demonstrated in the following chapter.

Omniscience. Matt. xi. 27, 'all things are
delivered unto me of my Father, and no man
knoweth the Son, but the Father, neither knoweth
any man the Father, save the Son, and he to
whomsoever the Son will reveal him.' John v.
20, 'the Father loveth the Son, and sheweth him
all things'; viii. 26, 'I speak those things that
I have heard of him'; v. 28, 'then shall ye know
that . . . as my Father hath taught me, I speak
these things'; v. 38, 'I speak that which I have
seen with my Father'; xv. 15, 'all things that
I have heard of my Father, I have made known

unto you '; ii. 24, 25, 'he knew all men . . for he knew what was in man'; xxi. 17, 'thou knowest all things'; xvi. 30, 'now are we sure that thou knowest all things . . . by this we believe that thou camest forth from God'; iii. 31–34, 'he that cometh from heaven . . . what he hath seen and heard . . . he whom God hath sent speaketh the words of God; for God giveth not the Spirit by measure unto him.' Rev. i. 1, 'the revelation of Jesus Christ, which God gave unto him'—whence it is written of him, ii. 23, 'I am he which searcheth the reins and hearts,' —even as it is said of the faithful, that they know all things; I John ii. 20, 'ye have an unction from the Holy One, and ye know all things.' Even the Son, however, knows not all things absolutely; there being some secret purposes, the knowledge of which the Father has reserved to himself alone. Mark xiii. 32, 'of that day and that hour knoweth no man, no, not the angels which are in heaven, neither the Son, but the Father'; or as it is in Matt. xxiv. 36, 'my Father only.' Acts i. 7, 'the times and the seasons which the Father hath put in his own power.'

Authority. Matt. xxviii. 18, 'all power is given unto me in heaven and in earth.' Luke xxii. 29, 'I appoint unto you a kingdom, as my Father hath appointed unto me.' John v. 22, 'the Father hath committed all judgment unto the Son '; v. 43, 'I am come in my Father's name'; vii. 16, 'my doctrine is not mine, but his that sent me'; viii. 42, 'I proceeded forth and came from God; neither came I of myself, but he sent me'; xii. 49, 50, 'I have not spoken of myself, but the Father which sent me, he gave me a commandment what I should say, and what I should speak'; xiv. 24, 'the word which ye hear is not mine, but the Father's which sent me'; xvii. 2, 'as thou hast given him power over all flesh.' Rev. ii. 26, 27, 'to him will I give power . . . even as I received of my Father.'

Omnipotence. John v. 19, 'the Son can do nothing of himself, but what he seeth the Father do; for what things soever he doeth, these also doeth the Son likewise'; v. 30, 'I can of my own self do nothing'; x. 18, 'I have power to lay it down, and I have power to take it again: this commandment have I received of my Father.' Hence Philipp. iii. 21, 'he is able even to subdue all things unto himself.' Rev. i. 8, 'I am . . . the Almighty': though it may be questioned whether this is not said of God the Father by the Son or the angel representing his authority, as has been explained before: so also Psalm ii. 7.

Works. John v. 20, 21, 'for the Father will shew him greater works than these . . . for as the Father raiseth up the dead, and quickeneth them; even so the Son quickeneth whom he will';

v. 36, ' the works that my Father hath given me to finish, the same works that I do, bear witness of me that the Father hath sent me ':—it is not therefore his divinity of which they bear witness, but his mission from God ; and so in other places. viii. 28, ' then shall ye know that I am he, and that I do nothing of myself ' ; x. 32, ' many good works have I shewed you from my Father ' ; xi. 22, ' I know that even now, whatsoever thou wilt ask of God, God will give it thee ' ; v. 41, ' Father, I thank thee that thou hast heard me.' So likewise in working miracles, even where he does not expressly implore the divine assistance, he nevertheless acknowledges it. Matt. xii. 28 compared with Luke xi. 20, ' I cast out devils by the Spirit, or finger, of God.' John xiv. 10, ' the Father that dwelleth in me, he doeth the works.' Yet the nature of these works, although divine, was such, that angels were not precluded from performing similar miracles at the same time and in the same place where Christ himself abode daily : John v. 4, ' an angel went down at a certain season into the pool.' The disciples also performed the same works. John xiv. 12, ' he that believeth on me, the works that I do shall he do also ; and greater works than these shall he do.'

The following gifts also, great as they are, were received by him from the Father. First, the power of conversion. John vi. 44, ' no man can come to me, except the Father which hath sent me draw him'; xvii. 2, 'that he should give eternal life to as many as thou hast given him'; and so uniformly; whence arises the expression, Matt. xxiv. 31—'his elect.' Wherever therefore Christ is said to have chosen any one, as John xiii. 18 and xv. 16, 19, he must be understood to speak only of the election to the apostolical office.

Secondly, creation—but with this peculiarity, that it is always said to have taken place *per eum*, through him, not by him, but by the Father. Isa. li. 16, 'I have put my words in thy mouth, and I have covered thee in the shadow of mine hand, that I may plant the heavens, and lay the foundations of the earth, and say unto Zion, Thou art my people.' Whether this be understood of the old or the new creation, the inference is the same. Rom. xi. 36, 'for of him' (*ex eo*)—that is, of the Father—'and through him (*per eum*), and to him, are all things; to whom be glory for ever.' I Cor. viii. 6, 'to us there is but one God, the Father, of whom (*a quo*) are all things, and we in him; and one Lord Jesus Christ, by whom (*per quem*) are all things.'[1] But the preposition *per* must signify the secondary efficient cause, whenever the *efficiens a quo*, that is, the principal efficient cause, is either expressed

---

[1] The remaining passages on the same subject are cited in Chap. VII, treatise 'On Christian Doctrine.'

or understood. Now it appears from all the texts
which have been already quoted, as well as from
those which will be produced hereafter, that the
Father is the first or chief cause of all things.
This is evident even from the single passage,
Heb. iii. 1–6, 'consider the Apostle . . . who
was faithful to him that appointed him . . . who
hath builded the house,' that is, the Church.
But he 'that appointed him,' v. 2, and 'builded
all things, is God,' that is, the Father, v. 4.

Thirdly, the remission of sins, even in his
human nature. John v. 22, 'the Father hath
committed all judgment unto the Son.' Matt.
ix. 6, 'that ye may know that the Son of man
hath power on earth to forgive sins, then saith
he,' etc. Acts v. 31, 'him hath God exalted with
his right hand to be a Prince and a Saviour, for
to give repentance to Israel, and forgiveness of
sins.' Hence Stephen says, vii. 60, 'Lord, lay
not this sin to their charge.' It clearly appears
from these passages that the following expression
in Isaiah refers primarily to God the Father,
xxxv. 4–6, 'behold, your God will come with
vengeance, even God with a recompense, he will
come and save you : then the eyes of the blind
shall be opened,' etc. For it was the Father
who appointed Christ 'to be a Saviour,' Acts
v. 31, and the Father is said 'to come unto him,'
John xiv. 23, and 'do the works,' as has been
proved before.

Fourthly, preservation. John xvii. 11, 12, 'holy Father, keep through thine own name those whom thou hast given me . . . I kept them in thy name'; v. 15, 'I pray . . . that thou shouldest keep them from the evil.' Col. i. 17, 'by him all things consist.' Heb. i. 3, 'upholding all things by the word of his power,' where it is read in the Greek, not *of his own power*, but 'of his,' namely, of the Father's power.[1]

Fifthly, renovation. Acts v. 31, 'him hath God exalted with his right hand, to be a Prince and a Saviour, for to give repentance to Israel.' I Cor. i. 30, 'of him are ye in Christ Jesus, who of God is made unto us wisdom, and righteousness, and sanctification, and redemption.' II Cor. iv. 6, 'for God, who commanded the light to shine out of darkness, hath shined in our hearts to give the light of the knowledge of the glory of God in the face of Jesus Christ'; v. 17-21, 'behold, all things are become new, and all things are of God, who hath reconciled himself to us

[1] This subject is considered again by Milton in Chap. VIII of the treatise 'On Christian Doctrine,' dealing with Providence, where the chief government of all things is shown 'to belong primarily to the Father alone ; whence the Father, Jehovah, is often called by the prophets not only the Preserver, but also the Saviour. Those who refer these passages to the Son, on account of the appellation of Saviour, seem to conceive that they hereby gain an important argument for his divinity ; as if the same title were not frequently applied to the Father in the New Testament.' See also Chap. XIII.

by Jesus Christ . . . we pray you in Christ's
stead, be ye reconciled unto God : for he hath
made him to be sin for us, who knew no sin, that
we might be made the righteousness of God in
him.' Hence Jer. xxiii. 6 may be explained
without difficulty : ' this is his name whereby he
shall be called Jehovah our righteousness,' and
xxxiii. 16, ' this is the name wherewith she shall
be called ' (that is, the Church, which does not
thereby become essentially one with God) ' Jehovah our righteousness.'

Sixthly, the power of conferring gifts—namely,
that vicarious power which he has received from
the Father. John xvii. 18, ' as thou hast sent
me into the world, even so have I also sent them
into the world.' See also xx. 21. Hence Matt.
x. 1, ' he gave them power against unclean
spirits.' Acts iii. 6, ' in the name of Jesus Christ
of Nazareth, rise up and walk ' ; ix. 34, ' Jesus
Christ maketh thee whole.' What was said before
of his works, may be repeated here. John xiv.
16, ' I will pray the Father, and he shall give
you another Comforter ' ; xvi. 13, etc., ' the Spirit
shall receive of mine . . . all things that the
Father hath are mine, therefore said I that he shall
take of mine ' ; xx. 21, 22, ' as my Father hath
sent me, even so send I you . . . receive the
Holy Ghost.' Hence Eph. iv. 8, ' he gave gifts
to men ' ; compared with Psalm lxviii. 18 whence
it is taken—' thou hast received gifts for men.'

Seventhly, his mediatorial work itself, or rather his passion. Matt. xxvi. 39, 'O my Father, if it be possible, let this cup pass from me.' Luke xxii. 43, 'there appeared an angel unto him from heaven, strengthening him.' Heb. v. 7, 8, 'who in the days of his flesh, when he had offered up prayers and supplications with strong crying and tears unto him that was able to save him from death, and was heard in that he feared : though he were a Son, yet learned he obedience by the things which he suffered.' For if the Son was able to accomplish by his own independent power the work of his passion, why did he forsake himself ; why did he implore the assistance of his Father ; why was an angel sent to strengthen him ? How then can the Son be considered co-essential and co-equal with the Father ? So too he exclaimed upon the cross—'My God, my God, why hast thou forsaken me ? ' He whom the Son, himself God, addresses as God, must be the Father—why then did the Son call upon the Father ? Because he felt even his divine nature insufficient to support him under the pains of death. Thus also he said, when at the point of death, Luke xxiii. 46, 'Father, into thy hands I commend my spirit.' To whom rather than to himself as God would he have commended himself in his human nature, if by his own divine nature alone he had possessed sufficient power to deliver himself from death ? It was therefore the Father only who raised him again to life ; which is the next particular to be noticed.

Eighthly, his resuscitation from death. II Cor. iv. 14, 'knowing that he which raised up the Lord Jesus, shall raise up us also by Jesus, and shall present us with you.' I Thess. iv. 14, 'them also which sleep in Jesus shall God bring with him.' But this point has been sufficiently illustrated by ample quotations in a former part of the chapter.

Ninthly, his future judicial advent. Rom. ii. 16, 'in the day when God shall judge the secrets of men by Jesus Christ according to my gospel.' I Tim. vi. 14, 'until the appearing of our Lord Jesus Christ.'

Tenthly, divine honours. John v. 22, 23, 'the Father hath committed all judgment unto the Son ; that all men should honour the Son, even as they honour the Father . . . which hath sent him.' Philipp. ii. 9–11, 'God hath highly exalted him, and hath given him a name . . . that at the name of Jesus every knee should bow and that every tongue should confess that Jesus Christ is Lord, to the glory of God the Father.' Heb. i. 6, 'when he bringeth in the first-begotten into the world, he saith, And let all the angels of God worship him.' Rev. v. 12, 'worthy is the Lamb that was slain to receive power,' etc. Hence Acts vii. 59, 'calling upon God, and saying, Lord Jesus, receive my spirit ' ;

ix. 14, 'all that call upon thy name.' I Cor. i. 2, 'with all that in every place call upon the name of Jesus Christ our Lord.' II Tim. ii. 22, 'with them that call upon the Lord out of a pure heart,' that is, as it is explained Col. iii. 17, 'whatsoever ye do . . . do it in the name of the Lord Jesus, giving thanks to God and the Father by him.' II Tim. ii. 19, 'every one that nameth the name of Christ.' It appears therefore that when we call upon the Son of God, it is only in his capacity of advocate with the Father. So Rev. xxii. 20, 'even so, come, Lord Jesus'—namely, to execute judgment, 'which the Father hath committed unto him, that all men might honour the Son,' etc., John v. 22, 23.

Eleventhly, baptism in his name. Matt. xxviii. 18, 19, 'all power is given unto me in heaven and in earth ; go ye therefore and teach all nations, baptizing them in the name of the Father, and of the Son, and of the Holy Ghost.' More will be said on this subject in the next chapter.

Twelfthly, belief in him ; if indeed this ought to be considered as an honour peculiar to divinity ; for the Israelites are said, Exod. xiv. 31, 'to believe Jehovah and his servant Moses.' Again, 'to believe the prophets' occurs II Chron. xx. 20, and 'faith toward all saints,' Philem. 5, and 'Moses in whom ye trust,' John v. 45. Whence it would seem, that *to believe in any one* is nothing more than an Hebraism, which the Greeks or

Latins express by the phrase *to believe any one*;
so that whatever trifling distinction may be made
between the two, originates in the schools, and
not in Scripture. For in some cases *to believe
in any one* implies no faith at all. John ii. 23, 24,
'many believed in his name . . but Jesus did
not commit himself unto them'; xii. 42, 'many
believed on him, but because of the Pharisees
they did not confess him.' On the other hand,
to believe any one often signifies the highest degree
of faith. John v. 24, 'he that believeth on him
(*qui credit ei*) that sent me, hath everlasting life.'
Rom. iv. 3, 'Abraham believed God, and it was
counted unto him for righteousness.' I John v.
10, 'he that believeth not God.' See also Titus
iii. 8. This honour, however, like the others, is
derived from the Father. John iii. 35, 36, 'the
Father hath given all things into his hand: he
that believeth on the Son hath everlasting life';
vi. 40, 'this is the will of him that sent me, that
every one which seeth the Son, and believeth on
him, may have everlasting life'; xii. 44, 'Jesus
cried and said, He that believeth on me, believeth
not on me, but on him that sent me.' Hence
xiv. 1, 'ye that believe in God, believe also in
me.' I John iii. 23, 'this is his commandment,
that we should believe on the name of his Son
Jesus Christ.' It may therefore be laid down as
certain, that *believing in Christ* implies nothing
more than that we believe Christ to be the Son

of God, sent from the Father for our salvation. John xi. 25–27, 'Jesus said unto her, I am the resurrection and the life ; he that believeth in me though he were dead, yet shall he live : and whosoever liveth and believeth in me shall never die. Believest thou this ? She saith unto him, Yea, Lord ; I believe that thou art the Christ, the Son of God, which should come into the world.'

Thirteenthly, divine glory. John i. 1, 'the Word was with God, and the Word was God' ; v. 14, 'we beheld his glory, the glory as of the only-begotten of the Father,' παρὰ Πατρός· v. 18, 'no man hath seen God at any time ; the only-begotten Son, which is in the bosom of the Father, he hath declared him' ; vi. 46, 'not that any man hath seen the Father, save he which is of God,' ὁ ὢν παρὰ τοῦ Θεοῦ ; xvii. 5, 'glorify thou me with thine own self with the glory which I had with thee before the world was.' No one doubts that the Father restored the Son, on his ascent into heaven, to that original place of glory of which he here speaks. That place will be universally acknowledged to be the right hand of God ; the same therefore was his place of glory in the beginning, and from which he had descended. But the right hand of God primarily signifies a glory, not in the highest sense divine, but only next in dignity to God. So v. 24, 'that they may behold my glory which thou hast given me; for thou lovedst me before the foundation of the world.' In these, as in other passages, we are taught that the nature of the Son is indeed divine, but distinct from and clearly inferior to the nature of the Father,—for to be with God, πρὸς Θεὸν, and to be from God, παρὰ Θεῷ,—to be God, and to be in the bosom of God the Father—to be God, and to be from God—to be the one invisible God, and to be the only-begotten and visible, are things so different that they cannot be predicated of one and the same essence. Besides, considering that his glory even in his divine nature before the foundation of the world, was not self-derived, but given by the love of the Father, he is plainly demonstrated to be inferior to the Father. So Matt. xvi. 27, 'in the glory of his Father.' Acts iii. 13, 'the God of Abraham, and of Isaac, and of Jacob, the God of our fathers, hath glorified his Son Jesus.' Col. i. 19, 'it pleased the Father that in him should all fulness dwell'; ii. 9, 'in him dwelleth all the fulness of the Godhead bodily.' Eph. iii. 19, 'that ye might be filled with all the fulness of God.' These passages most clearly evince that Christ has received his fulness from God, in the sense in which we shall receive our fulness from Christ. For the term 'bodily,' which is subjoined, either means *substantially*, in opposition to the 'vain deceit' mentioned in the preceding verse, or is of no weight in proving that Christ

H

is of the same essence with God. I Pet. i. 21, 'who gave him glory, that your faith and hope might be in God'; ii. 4, 'chosen of God and precious.' II Pet. i. 16, 17, 'we were eye-witnesses of his majesty; for he received from God the Father honour and glory, when there came such a voice to him—.' I Pet. iv. 11 compared with II Pet. iii. 18, 'that God in all things may be glorified, through Jesus Christ, to whom be praise and dominion for ever and ever : but grow in grace, and in the knowledge of our Lord and Saviour Jesus Christ ; to whom be glory both now and for ever.' On a collation of the two passages, it would seem that the phrase ' our Lord,' in the latter, must be understood of the Father, as is frequently the case. If, however, it be applied to the Son, the inference is the same, for it does not alter the doctrine of the former passage. John xii. 41, citing Isa. vi. 3. 5, ' these things said Esaias, when he saw his glory, and spake of him,'—that is, the glory of the only-begotten, given to the Son by the Father. Nor is any difficulty created by Isa xlii. 8, ' I am Jehovah, that is my name ; and my glory will I not give to another, neither my praise to graven images.' For though the Son be ' another ' than the Father, God only means that he will not give his glory to graven images and strange gods— not that he will not give it to the Son, who is the brightness of his glory, and the express image of his person, and upon whom he had promised that he would put his spirit, v. 1. For the Father does not alienate his glory from himself in imparting it to the Son, inasmuch as the Son uniformly glorifies the Father. John xiii. 31, 'now is the Son of man glorified, and God is glorified in him'; viii. 50, 'I seek not mine own glory; there is one that seeketh and judgeth.'

Hence it becomes evident on what principle the attributes of the Father are said to pertain to the Son. John xvi. 15, 'all things that the Father hath are mine'; xvii. 6, 7, 'thine they were, and thou gavest them me; . . . now they have known that all things whatsoever thou hast given me are of thee.' It is therefore said, v. 10, 'all mine are thine, and thine are mine'—namely, in the same sense in which he had called the kingdom his, Luke xxii. 30, for he had said in the preceding verse, 'I appoint unto you a kingdom, as my Father hath appointed unto me.'

Lastly, his coming to judgment. I Tim. vi. 14-16, 'until the appearing of our Lord Jesus Christ, which in his time he shall shew, who is the blessed and only Potentate, the King of kings and Lord of lords; who only hath immortality, dwelling in the light which no man can approach unto; whom no man hath seen, nor can see.'

Christ therefore, having received all these things from the Father, and 'being in the form of God, thought it not robbery to be equal with God,' Philipp. ii. 6, namely, because he had obtained them by gift, not by robbery. For if this passage imply his co-equality with the Father, it rather refutes than proves his unity of essence; since equality cannot exist but between two or more essences. Further, the phrases 'he did not think it'—'he made himself of no reputation' (literally, 'he emptied himself') appear inapplicable to the supreme God. For *to think* is nothing else than to entertain an opinion, which cannot be properly said of God. Nor can the infinite God be said to empty himself, any more than to contradict himself; for infinity and emptiness are opposite terms. But since he emptied himself of that form of God in which he had previously existed, if the form of God is to be taken for the essence of the Deity itself, it would prove him to have emptied himself of that essence, which is impossible.

Again, the Son himself acknowledges and declares openly, that the Father is greater than the Son; which was the last proposition I undertook to prove. John x. 29, 'My Father is greater than all'; xiv. 28, 'my Father is greater than I.' It will be answered, that Christ is speaking of his human nature. But did his disciples understand him as speaking merely of his human nature? Was this the belief in himself which

Christ required ? Such an opinion will scarcely be maintained. If therefore he said this, not of his human nature only (for that the Father was greater than he in his human nature could not admit of a doubt), but in the sense in which he himself wished his followers to conceive of him both as God and man, it ought undoubtedly to be understood as if he had said, My Father is greater than I, whatsoever I am, both in my human and divine nature ; otherwise the speaker would not have been he in whom they believed, and instead of teaching them, he would only have been imposing upon them with an equivocation. He must therefore have intended to compare the nature with the person, not the nature of God the Father with the nature of the Son in his human form. So v. 31, ' as the Father gave me commandment, even so I do.' John v. 18, 19. Being accused by the Jews of having made himself equal with God, he expressly denies it : ' the Son can do nothing of himself,' v. 30, ' as I hear I judge, and my judgment is just ; because I seek not mine own will, but the will of my Father which sent me ' ; vi. 38, ' I came down from heaven, not to do mine own will, but the will of him that sent me.' Now he that was sent was the only begotten Son ; therefore the will of the Father is other and greater than the will of the only begotten Son. vii. 28, ' Jesus cried in the temple, saying . . . I am not come of myself ' ; viii. 29,

' he that sent me is with me : the Father hath not
left me alone ; for I do always those things
that please him.' If he says this as God, how
could he be left by the Father, with whom he
was essentially one ? if as man, what is meant
by his being 'left alone,' who was sustained by a
Godhead of equal power ? And why ' did not
the Father leave him alone ' ?—not because he
was essentially one with him, but because he ' did
always those things that pleased him,' that is, as
the less conforms himself to the will of the greater.
v. 42, ' neither came I of myself '—not therefore
of his own Godhead—' but he sent me ' · he that
sent him was therefore another and greater than
himself ; v. 49, ' I honour my Father ' ; v. 50,
' I seek not mine own glory ' ; v. 54, ' if I honour
myself, my glory is nothing ' ; it is therefore
less than the Father's glory.   x. 24, 25, ' if thou be
the Christ, tell us plainly .   the works that I
do in my Father's name, they bear witness of me.'
xv. 10, ' as I have kept my Father's commandments, and abide in his love.'   xvi. 25, ' the time
cometh when I shall no more speak to you in
proverbs, but I shall shew you plainly of the
Father.'   xx. 17, ' I ascend unto my Father
and your Father ; and to my God and your God.'
Compare also Rev. i. 11, ' I am Alpha and Omega,'
and v. 17, ' I am the first and the last.'   See also
ii. 8, iii. 12, ' him that overcometh will I make a
pillar in the temple of my God,' which is repeated

three times successively. Here he, who had just
before styled himself ' the first and the last,'
acknowledges that the Father was his God.
Matt. xi. 25, 26, ' I thank thee, O Father, Lord
of heaven and earth; because thou hast hid
these things, etc., even so, Father, for so it
seemed good in thy sight.'

Thus far we have considered the testimony of
the Son respecting the Father; let us now enquire
what is the testimony of the Father respecting
the Son: for it is written, Matt. xi. 27, ' no man
knoweth the Son, but the Father; neither
knoweth any man the Father, save the Son, and
he to whomsoever the Son will reveal him.'
I John v. 9, ' this is the witness of God which
he hath testified of his Son.' Here the Father,
when about to testify of the Son, is called God
absolutely; and his witness is most explicit.
Matt. iii. 17, ' this is my beloved Son, in whom
I am well pleased.' Isa. xlii. 1, compared with
Matt. xii. 18, ' behold my servant, whom I uphold;
mine elect, in whom my soul delighteth; I have
put my spirit upon him ' :—see also Matt. xvii. 5.
II Pet. i. 17, ' for he received from God the Father
honour and glory, when there came such a voice
to him from the excellent glory, This is my beloved Son, in whom I am well pleased.' Mal.
iii. 1, ' even the messenger of the covenant, behold
he shall come, saith Jehovah of hosts '; and still
more clearly Psalm ii. where God the Father is

introduced in his own person as explicitly declaring the nature and offices of his Son. Psalm ii. 7, 8, 11, 12, ' I will declare the decree ; Jehovah hath said unto me, Thou art my Son . . . ask of me and I shall give   serve Jehovah . . . kiss the Son.' Heb. i. 8, 9, ' unto the Son he saith, Thy throne, O God, is for ever and ever thou hast loved righteousness, and hated iniquity ; therefore God, even thy God, hath anointed thee with the oil of gladness above thy fellows.' To the above may also be added the testimony of the angel Gabriel, Luke i. 32, ' he shall be great, and shall be called the Son of the Highest, and the Lord God shall give unto him the throne of his father David.' If, then, he be the Son of the Most High, he is not himself the Most High.

The apostles everywhere teach the same doctrine ; as the Baptist had done before them. John i. 29, ' behold the Lamb of God ' ; v. 33, 34, ' I knew him not, but he that sent me to baptize with water, the same said unto me, etc., and I saw, and bare record that this is the Son of God ' ; iii. 32, ' what he hath seen and heard, that he testifieth,' etc.—not he alone that was 'earthly,' nor did he speak only of 'earthly things,' but he that is 'above all,' and that 'cometh from heaven,' v. 31, lest it should be still contended that this and similar texts refer to the human nature of Christ. II Cor. iv. 4, 6, ' lest the light of the glorious gospel of Christ, who is the image of God, should

shine unto them.' Col. i. 15, 'who is the image
of the invisible God, the first-born of every
creature.' Phil. ii. 6, 'in the form of God.' Heb.
i. 2, 'whom he hath appointed heir'; v. 3, 'the
brightness of his glory, and the express image of
his person.' The terms here used, being all
relative, and applied numerically to two persons,
prove, first, that there is no unity of essence,
and secondly, that the one is inferior to the
other. So v. 4, 'being made so much better than
the angels, as he hath by inheritance obtained
a more excellent name than they.' I Cor. iii. 23,
'ye are Christ's and Christ is God's.' Here, if
anywhere, it might have been expected that
Christ would have been designated by the title of
God; yet it is only said that he is 'of God.' The
same appears even more clearly in what follows:
xi. 3, 'I would have you know that . . . the
head of Christ is God.' Eph. i. 17, 'the God of
our Lord Jesus Christ.' I Cor. xv. 27, 'when he
saith, all things are put under him, it is manifest
that he is excepted, which did put all things
under him: and when all things shall be subdued
unto him, then shall the Son also himself be
subject unto him that put all things under him,
that God may be all in all.' Here the usual
subterfuge of the opponents of this doctrine, that
of alleging the mediatorial office of Christ, can
be of no avail; since it is expressly declared,
that when the Son shall have completed his

functions as mediator, and nothing shall remain
to prevent him from resuming his original glory
as only begotten Son, he shall nevertheless be
subject unto the Father.

Such was the faith of the saints respecting the
Son of God; such is the tenor of the celebrated
confession of that faith; such is the doctrine
which alone is taught in Scripture, which is
acceptable to God, and has the promise of eternal
salvation. Matt. xvi. 15-18, 'whom say ye that
I am? and Simon Peter answered and said,
Thou art the Christ, the Son of the living God:
and Jesus answered and said unto him: Blessed
art thou, Simon Bar-jona; for flesh and blood
hath not revealed it unto thee, but my Father
which is in heaven . . . upon this rock I will
build my Church.' Luke ix. 20, 'the Christ of
God.' John i. 49, 50, 'Nathanael answered and
saith unto him, Rabbi, thou art the Son of God;
thou art the King of Israel.' vi. 69, 'we believe
and are sure that thou art that Christ, the Son of
the living God.' ix. 35-38, 'dost thou believe
on the Son of God? he answered and said, Who
is he, Lord, that I might believe on him? and
Jesus said unto him, Thou hast both seen him,
and it is he that talketh with thee: and he said,
Lord, I believe; and he worshipped him.' xi.
22, 26, 27, 'I know that even now, whatsoever
thou wilt ask of God, God will give it thee:
whosoever liveth and believeth in me, shall never

die : believest thou this ? she saith unto him,
Yea, Lord, I believe that thou art the Christ,
the Son of God, which should come into the
world.' xvi. 27, 30, 31, 'the Father himself
loveth you, because ye have loved me, and have
believed that I came out from God : now are we
sure that thou knowest all things ; by this we
believe that thou camest forth from God.' xvii.
3, 7, 8, 21, 'this is life eternal that they might
know thee the only true God, and Jesus Christ
whom thou hast sent : now they have known
that all things, whatsoever thou hast given me,
are of thee ; for I have given unto them the
words which thou gavest me ; and they have
received them, and have known surely that I
came out from thee : that the world may believe
that thou hast sent me.' xx. 31, 'these are
written, that ye might believe that Jesus is the
Christ, the Son of God, and that believing, ye
might have life through his name.' Acts viii. 37,
'if thou believest, thou mayest . . . I believe
that Jesus Christ is the Son of God.' Rom. x. 9,
'if thou shalt believe in thine heart that God
hath raised him from the dead, thou shalt be
saved.' Col. ii. 2, 'that their hearts might be
comforted, being knit together in love, and unto
all riches of the full assurance of understanding,
to the acknowledgment of the mystery of God,
and of the Father, and of Christ.' Phil. iv. 6, 7,
'let your requests be made known unto God :

and the peace of God, which passeth all understanding, shall keep your hearts and minds
through Christ Jesus.'   I Pet. i. 21, ' who by him
do believe in God, that raised him up from the
dead, and gave him glory ; that your faith and
hope might be in God.'   I John iv. 15, ' whosoever shall confess that Jesus is the Son of God,
God dwelleth in him, and he in God ' ; v. 1,
' whosoever believeth that Jesus is the Christ,
is born of God ' ; v. 5, ' who is he that overcometh the world, but he that believeth that
Jesus is the Son of God ? '   Finally, this is the
faith proposed to us in the Apostles' Creed, the
most ancient and universally received com-
pendium of belief in the possession of the Church.

OF THE HOLY SPIRIT

HAVING concluded what relates to the Father and the Son, the next subject to be discussed is that of the Holy Spirit, inasmuch as this latter is called the Spirit of the Father and the Son. With regard to the nature of the Spirit, in what manner it exists, or whence it arose, Scripture is silent; which is a caution to us not to be too hasty in our conclusions on the subject. For though it be a Spirit, in the same sense in which the Father and Son are properly called Spirits; though we read that Christ by breathing on his disciples gave to them the Holy Ghost, or rather perhaps some symbol or pledge of the Holy Ghost, John xx. 22.—yet in treating of the nature of the Holy Spirit, we are not authorized to infer from such expressions, that the Spirit was breathed from the Father and the Son. The terms *emanation* and *procession* employed by theologians on the authority of John xv. 26, do not relate to the nature of the Holy Spirit; 'the Spirit of truth, ὃ παρὰ τοῦ Πατρὸς ἐκπορεύεται, who proceedeth or goeth forth from the Father'; which single expression is too slender a foundation for the full establishment of so great a mystery, especially as these words relate rather to the mission than to the nature of the Spirit; in which sense the Son also is often said ἐξελθεῖν, which in my opinion may be translated either ' to go forth ' or to ' proceed ' from the Father, without making any difference in the meaning. Nay, we are even said ' to live by every word (ἐκπορευομένῳ) that proceedeth, *or* goeth forth from the mouth of God,' Matt. iv. 4. Since therefore the Spirit is neither said to be generated nor created, nor is any other mode of existence specifically attributed to it in Scripture, we must be content to leave undetermined a point on which the sacred writers have preserved so uniform a silence.

The name of Spirit is also frequently applied to God and angels, and to the human mind. When the phrase, the Spirit of God, or the Holy Spirit, occurs in the Old Testament, it is to be variously interpreted; sometimes it signifies God the Father himself—as Gen. vi. 3, ' my Spirit shall not always strive with man '; sometimes the power and virtue of the Father, and particularly that divine breath or influence by which everything is created and nourished. In this sense many both of the ancient and modern interpreters understand the passage in Gen. i. 2, ' the Spirit of God moved upon the face of the waters.' Here, however, it appears to be used with refer-

ence, to the Son, through whom the Father is
so often said to have created all things. Job
xxvi. 13, 'by his Spirit he hath garnished the
heavens'; xxvii. 3, 'the Spirit of God is in my
nostrils'; xxxiii. 4, 'the Spirit of God hath made
me, and the breath of the Almighty hath given
me life.' Psalm civ. 30, 'thou sendest forth thy
Spirit, they are created'; cxxxix. 7, 'whither
shall I go from thy Spirit?' Ezek. xxxvii. 14,
'I shall put my Spirit in you, and ye shall
live.' See also many other similar passages.

Sometimes it means an angel. Isai. xlviii. 16,
'the Lord Jehovah and his Spirit hath sent me.'
Ezek. iii. 12, 'then the Spirit took me up.' See
also v. 14, 24, etc.

Sometimes it means Christ, who according to
the common opinion was sent by the Father to
lead the Israelites into the land of Canaan. Isa.
lxiii. 10, 11, 'they rebelled and vexed his Holy
Spirit . . . where is he that put his Holy Spirit
within them?'—that is, the angel to whom he
transferred his own name, namely, Christ 'whom
they tempted,' Num. xxi. 5, etc., compared with
I Cor. x. 9.

Sometimes it means that impulse or voice of
God by which the prophets were inspired. Neh.
ix. 30, 'thou testifiedst against them by thy
Spirit in thy prophets.'

Sometimes it means that light of truth, whether
ordinary or extraordinary, wherewith God en-

lightens and leads his people. Num. xiv. 24, 'my servant Caleb, because he had another Spirit within him—.' Neh. ix. 20, 'thou gavest also thy good Spirit to instruct them.' Psalm li. 11, 12, 'take not thy Holy Spirit from me . . . renew a right Spirit within me'; cxliii. 10, 'thy Spirit is good; lead me into the land of uprightness.' Undoubtedly neither David, nor any other Hebrew, under the old covenant, believed in the personality of that 'good' and 'Holy Spirit,' unless perhaps as an angel.

More particularly, it implies that light which was shed on Christ himself. Isai. xi. 2, 'the Spirit of Jehovah shall rest upon him, the Spirit of wisdom and understanding, the Spirit of counsel and might, the Spirit of knowledge and of the fear of Jehovah'; xlii. 1, 'I have put my Spirit upon him,' compared with Acts x. 38, 'how God anointed Jesus of Nazareth with the Holy Ghost and with power.'

It is also used to signify the spiritual gifts conferred by God on individuals, and the act of gift itself. Gen. xli. 38, 'a man in whom the Spirit of God is.' Num. xi. 17, 25, 26, 29, 'I will take of the Spirit which is upon thee, and will put it upon them.' II Kings ii. 9, 'I pray thee, let a double portion of thy Spirit be upon me'; v. 15, 'the Spirit of Elijah doth rest upon Elisha.'

Nothing can be more certain than that all these passages, and many others of a similar kind in

the Old Testament, were understood of the virtue
and power of God the Father, inasmuch as the
Holy Spirit was not yet given, nor believed in,
even by those who prophesied that it should be
poured forth in the latter times.

So likewise under the Gospel, what is called the
Holy Spirit, or the Spirit of God, sometimes means
the Father himself. Matt. i. 18, 20, ' that which
is conceived in her is of the Holy Ghost.' Luke
i. 35, ' the Holy Ghost shall come upon thee,
and the power of the Highest shall overshadow
thee ; therefore also that holy thing which shall
be born of thee, shall be called the Son of God.'

Again, it sometimes means the virtue and
power of the Father. Matt. xii. 28 compared
with Luke xi. 20, ' I cast out devils by the Spirit
or finger of God.' Rom. i. 4, ' declared to be the
Son of God with power, according to the Spirit
of holiness, by the resurrection from the dead.'
For thus the Scripture teaches throughout, that
Christ was raised by the power of the Father,
and thereby declared to be the Son of God. See
particularly Acts xiii. 32, 33, quoted in the
beginning of the last chapter. But the phrase,
' according to the Spirit ' (*secundum Spiritum*)
seems to have the same signification as Eph. iv.
24, ' which after God (*secundum Deum*) is created
in righteousness and true holiness ' ; and I Pet.
iv. 6 ' that they might live according to God
(*secundum Deum*) in the Spirit.' Isai. xlii. 1,

compared with Heb. ix. 14, ' I have put my Spirit
upon him . . . who through the eternal Spirit
offered himself without spot to God.'   Luke iv. 1,
' Jesus, being full of the Holy Ghost,' and v. 18,
compared with Isai. lxi. 1, ' the Spirit of the Lord
Jehovah is upon me, because he hath anointed
me to preach the gospel to the poor ; he hath
sent me,' etc.   Acts x. 38, ' God anointed Jesus
of Nazareth with the Holy Ghost and with power ' ;
i. 2, ' after that he through the Holy Ghost had
given commandments unto the apostles whom
he had chosen.'   It is more probable that these
phrases are to be understood of the power of the
Father, than of the Holy Spirit himself ; for
how could it be necessary that Christ should be
filled with the Holy Spirit, of whom he had
himself said, John xvi. 15, ' he shall take of mine ' ?
For the same reason I am inclined to believe that
the Spirit descended upon Christ at his baptism,
not so much in his own name, as in virtue of a
mission from the Father, and as a symbol and
minister of the divine power.   For what could
the Spirit confer on Christ, from whom he was
himself to be sent, and to receive all things ?
Was his purpose to bear witness to Christ ?   But
as yet he was himself not so much as known.
Was it meant that the Spirit should be then
manifested for the first time to the church ?
But at the time of his appearance nothing was
said of him or of his office ; nor did that voice

from heaven bear any testimony to the Spirit, but only to the Son. The descent therefore and appearance of the Holy Spirit in the likeness of a dove, seems to have been nothing more than a representation of the ineffable affection of the Father for the Son, communicated by the Holy Spirit under the appropriate image of a dove, and accompanied by a voice from heaven declaratory of that affection.

Thirdly, the Spirit signifies a divine impulse, or light, or voice, or word, transmitted from above either through Christ, who is the Word of God, or by some other channel. Mark xii. 36, 'David himself said by the Holy Ghost.' Acts i. 16, 'the Holy Ghost by the mouth of David spake before concerning Judas'; xxviii. 25, 'well spake the Holy Ghost by Esaias the prophet.' Heb. iii. 7, 'wherefore, as the Holy Ghost saith, To-day if ye will hear his voice,' etc. ; ix. 8, 'the Holy Ghost this signifying, that the way into the holiest of all was not yet made manifest'; x. 15, 'whereof the Holy Ghost also is a witness to us.' II Pet. i. 21, 'holy men of God spake as they were moved by the Holy Ghost.' Luke ii. 25, 26, 'the Holy Ghost was upon him : and it was revealed unto him by the Holy Ghost'—. It appears to me, that these and similar passages cannot be considered as referring to the express person of the Spirit, both because the Spirit was not yet given, and because Christ alone, as has been said before, is, properly speaking, and in a primary sense, the Word of God, and the Prophet of the Church ; though ' God at sundry times and in divers manners spake in time past unto the fathers by the prophets,' Heb. i. 1, whence it appears that he did not speak by the Holy Spirit alone, unless the term be understood in the signification which I have proposed, and in a much wider sense than was subsequently attributed to it. Hence I Pet. i. 11, ' searching what or what manner of time the Spirit of Christ which was in them '—that is, in the prophets— ' did signify,' must either be understood of Christ himself—as iii. 18, 19, ' quickened by the Spirit, by which also he went and preached unto the spirits in prison '—or it must be understood of the Spirit which supplied the place of Christ the Word and the Chief Prophet.

Further, the Spirit signifies the person itself of the Holy Spirit, or its symbol. Matt. iii. 16, Mark i. 10, ' he saw the Spirit of God descending like a dove, and lighting upon him.' Luke iii. 22, ' in a bodily shape like a dove.' John i. 32, ' like a dove.' Nor let it be objected, that a dove is not a person ; for an intelligent substance, under any form whatever, is a person ; as, for instance, the four living creatures seen in Ezekiel's vision, ch. i. John xiv. 16, ' another Comforter.' See also xiv. 26, xv. 26, xvi. 7, 13. xx. 22, ' he breathed on them, and saith unto them,

Receive ye the Holy Ghost '—which is a kind of
symbol, and sure pledge of that promise, the
fulfilment of which is recorded, Acts ii. 2-4, 33,
'having received of the Father the promise of
the Holy Ghost, he hath shed forth this.' Matt.
xxviii. 19, 'in the name of the Father, and of
the Son, and of the Holy Ghost.' Acts xv. 28,
'it seemed good to the Holy Ghost.' Rom.
viii. 16, 'the Spirit itself beareth witness with our
spirit '; v. 26, 'it helpeth our infirmities . . .
it maketh intercession for us.' Eph. i. 13, 14,
τῷ πνεύματι τῷ ἁγίῳ, ὅς ἐστιν ἀῤῥαβών· 'ye were
sealed with that Holy Spirit of promise which
[who, Whitby, Macknight] is the earnest of our
inheritance '; iv. 30, 'grieve not the Holy Spirit
of God.'

Lastly, it signifies the donation of the Spirit
itself, and of its attendant gifts. John vii. 39,
'but this spake he of the Spirit, which they that
believe on him should receive ; for the Holy
Ghost was not yet given.' Matt. iii. 11, 'he
shall baptize you with the Holy Ghost and with
fire.' See also Acts i. 5 and xi. 16. I Thess.
v. 19,' quench not the Spirit.'

Who this Holy Spirit is, and whence he comes,
and what are his offices, no one has taught us
more explicitly than the Son of God himself,
Matt. x. 20, 'it is not ye that speak, but the
Spirit of your Father that speaketh in you.'
Luke xi. 13, 'how much more shall your heavenly

Father give the Holy Spirit to them that ask him ' ;
xxiv. 49, 'behold, I send the promise of my
Father upon you ; but tarry ye in the city of
Jerusalem, until ye be endued with power from
on high.' John xiv. 16, 17, 'I will pray the
Father, and he shall give you another Comforter,
that he may abide with you for ever, even the
Spirit of truth.' v. 26, 'the Comforter, which
is the Holy Ghost, whom the Father will send in
my name.' xv. 26, 'the Comforter whom I will
send unto you from the Father . . . which
proceedeth from the Father, he shall testify of
me.' xvi. 7, 'I will send him unto you.' v. 8,
'when he is come, he will reprove the world—.'
v. 13, 'he shall not speak of himself ; but whatsoever he shall hear, that shall he speak.' v. 14,
'he shall glorify me, for he shall receive of mine.'
v. 15, 'all things that the Father hath are mine ;
therefore said I that he shall take of mine.' xx.
22, 'when he had said this, he breathed on them,
and saith unto them, Receive ye the Holy Ghost.'
Acts ii. 2–4, 33, 'having received of the Father
the promise of the Holy Ghost, he hath shed forth
this—.' v. 32, 'we are his witnesses of these
things, and so is also the Holy Ghost whom
God hath given to them that obey him.' Rom.
xv. 13, 'now the God of hope fill you with all joy
and peace in believing, that ye may abound in
hope through the power of the Holy Ghost.'
I Cor. xii. 3, 'no man can say that Jesus is the

Lord, but by the Holy Ghost.' Heb. ii. 4, ' God
also bearing them witness both with signs and
wonders, and with divers miracles, and gifts of
the Holy Ghost, according to his own will.'
Hence he is called the Spirit of the Father, the
Spirit of God, and even the Spirit of Christ. Matt.
x. 20, ' it is the Spirit of your Father that speaketh
in you.' Rom. viii. 9, ' but ye are not in the flesh,
but in the Spirit, if so be that the Spirit of God
dwell in you: now if any man have not the
Spirit of Christ, he is none of his.' v. 15, 16,
' ye have received the Spirit of adoption, whereby
we cry ' Abba, Father ; the Spirit itself beareth
witness with our spirit, that we are the Sons of
God.' I Cor. vi. 11, ' by the Spirit of our God.'
II Cor. i. 21, 22, ' he which stablisheth us with
you in Christ, and hath anointed us, is God ;
who hath also sealed us, and given the earnest
of the Spirit in our hearts.' Gal. iv. 6, ' God
hath sent forth the Spirit of his Son into our
hearts, crying, Abba, Father.' Eph. i. 13, 14,
' that holy Spirit of promise, which is the earnest
of our inheritance ' ; iv. 30, ' grieve not the
holy Spirit of God, whereby ye are sealed ' ;
ii. 18, ' through him we both have access by one
Spirit unto the Father.' I Pet. i. 12, ' the Holy
Ghost sent down from heaven.' From all which
results the command in Matt. xxviii. 19, ' baptizing them in the name of the Father, and of
the Son, and of the Holy Ghost.' I John v. 7,

' there are three that bear witness in heaven, the Father, the Word, and the Holy Ghost ; and these three are one.' The latter passage has been considered in the preceding chapter ; but both will undergo a further examination in a subsequent part of the present.

If it be the divine will that a doctrine which is to be understood and believed as one of the primary articles of our faith, should be delivered without obscurity or confusion, and explained, as is fitting, in clear and precise terms—if it be certain that particular care ought to be taken in everything connected with religion, lest the objection urged by Christ against the Samaritans should be applicable to us—' ye worship ye know not what,' John iv. 22—if our Lord's saying should be held sacred wherever points of faith are in question—' we know what we worship '—the particulars which have been stated seem to contain all that we are capable of knowing, or are required to know respecting the Holy Spirit, inasmuch as revelation has declared nothing else expressly on the subject. The nature of these particulars is such, that although the Holy Spirit be nowhere said to have taken upon himself any mediatorial functions, as is said of Christ, nor to be engaged by the obligations of a filial relation to pay obedience to the Father, yet he must evidently be considered as inferior to both Father and Son, inasmuch as he is represented and declared to be subservient and obedient in all things ; to have been promised, and sent, and given ; to speak nothing of himself ; and even to have been given as an earnest. There is no room here for any sophistical distinction founded on a twofold nature ; all these expressions refer to the Holy Spirit, who is maintained to be the supreme God ; whence it follows, that wherever similar phrases are applied to the Son of God, in which he is distinctly declared to be inferior to the Father, they ought to be understood in reference to his divine as well to his human character. For what those, who believe in the Holy Spirit's co-equality with the Father, deem to be not unworthy of him, cannot be considered unworthy of the Son, however exalted may be the dignity of his Godhead. Wherefore it remains now to be seen on what grounds, and by what arguments, we are constrained to believe that the Holy Spirit is God, if Scripture nowhere expressly teach the doctrine of his divinity, not even in the passages where his office is explained at large, nor in those where the unity of God is explicitly asserted, as in John xvii. 3, I Cor. viii. 4, etc., nor where God is either described, or introduced as sitting upon his throne,—if, further, the Spirit be frequently named the Spirit of God, and the Holy Spirit of God, Eph. iv. 30, so that the Spirit of God being actually and numerically distinct from God himself, cannot possibly be essentially one God with him whose Spirit he is (except on certain strange and absurd hypotheses, which have no foundation in Holy Scripture, but were devised by human ingenuity, for the sole purpose of supporting this particular doctrine)—if, wherever the Father and the Holy Spirit are mentioned together, the Father alone be called God, and the Father alone, omitting all notice of the Spirit, be acknowledged by Christ himself to be the one true God, as has been proved in the former chapter by abundant testimony;— if he be God who 'stablisheth us in Christ,' who 'hath anointed us,' who 'hath sealed us,' and 'given us the earnest of the Spirit,' II Cor. i. 22, if that God be one God, and that one God the Father;—if, finally, 'God hath sent forth the Spirit of his Son into our hearts, crying, Abba, Father,' Gal. iv. 6, whence it follows that he who sent both the Spirit of his Son and the Son himself, he on whom we are taught to call, and on whom the Spirit himself calls, is the one God and the only Father; it remains to be seen in what way, and on what proofs, we are to believe that the Holy Spirit is God. It seems exceedingly unreasonable, not to say dangerous, that in a matter of so much difficulty, believers should be required to receive a doctrine, represented by its advocates as of primary importance and of undoubted certainty, on anything less than the clearest testimony of Scripture; and that a point

which is confessedly contrary to human reason,
should nevertheless, be considered as susceptible
of proof from human reason only, or rather from
doubtful and obscure disputations

First, then, it is usual to defend the divinity
of the Holy Spirit on the ground, that the name
of God seems to be attributed to the Spirit:
Acts v. 3, 4, 'why hath Satan filled thine heart
to lie to the Holy Ghost ? . . . thou hast not lied
unto men, but unto God.' But if attention be
paid to what has been stated before respecting the
Holy Ghost on the authority of the Son, this passage will appear too weak for the support of so
great a doctrinal mystery. For since the Spirit
is expressly said to be sent by the Father, and
in the name of the Son, he who lies to the Spirit
must lie to God, in the same sense as he who
receives an apostle, receives God who sent him,
Matt. x. 40, John xiii. 20. St. Paul himself
removes all ground of controversy from this
passage, and explains it most appositely by
implication, I Thess. iv. 8, where his intention is
evidently to express the same truth more at
large : 'he therefore that despiseth, despiseth
not man, but God, who hath also given unto us
his Holy Spirit.' Besides, it may be doubted
whether the Holy Spirit in this passage does not
signify God the Father; for Peter afterwards
says, Acts v. 9, 'how is it that ye have agreed
together to tempt the Spirit of the Lord ?' that

is, God the Father himself, and his divine intelligence, which no one can elude or deceive. And in Acts v. 32 the Holy Spirit is not called God, but a witness of Christ with the apostles, ' whom God hath given to them that obey him.' So also Acts ii. 38, ' ye shall receive the gift of the Holy Ghost,' the gift, that is, of God. But how can the gift of God be himself God, much more the supreme God ?

The second passage is Acts xxviii. 25, compared with Isai. vi. 8, 9, ' I heard the voice of the Lord saying—, etc. . . . well spake the Holy Ghost by Esaias the prophet,' etc. See also Jer. xxxi. 31, compared with Heb. x. 15. But it has been shewn above, that the names Lord and Jehovah are throughout the Old Testament attributed to whatever angel God may entrust with the execution of his commands ; and in the New Testament the Son himself openly testifies of the Holy Spirit, John xvi. 13, that ' he shall not speak of himself, but whatsoever he shall hear, that shall he speak.' It cannot therefore be inferred from this passage, any more than from the preceding, that the Holy Ghost is God.

The third place is I Cor. iii. 16, compared with vi. 19, and II Cor. vi. 16, ' the temple of God . . . the temple of the Holy Ghost.' But neither is it here said, nor does it in any way follow from hence, that the Holy Spirit is God ; for it is not because the Spirit alone, but because the Father also and the Son 'make their abode with us,' that we are called 'the temple of God.' Therefore in I Cor. vi. 19, where we are called 'the temple of the Holy Ghost,' St. Paul has added, 'which ye have of God,' as if with the purpose of guarding against any error which might arise respecting the Holy Spirit in consequence of his expression. How then can it be deduced from this passage, that he whom we have of God, is God himself? In what sense we are called 'the temple of the Holy Ghost,' the same apostle has explained more fully, Eph. ii. 22, 'in whom ye also are builded together for an habitation of God through the Spirit.'

The next evidence which is produced for this purpose, is the ascription of the divine attributes to the Spirit. And first, Omniscience; as if the Spirit were altogether of the same essence with God. I Cor. ii. 10, 11, 'the Spirit searcheth all things, yea the deep things of God: for what man knoweth the things of a man, save the spirit of man which is in him? even so the things of God knoweth no man, but the Spirit of God.' With regard to the tenth verse, I reply, that in the opinion of divines, the question here is not respecting the divine omniscience, but only respecting those deep things 'which God hath revealed unto us by his Spirit'—the words immediately preceding. Besides, the phrase 'all things' must be restricted to mean whatever it is expedient for us to know: not to mention that it would be absurd to speak of God searching God, with whom he was one is essence. Next, as to the eleventh verse, the essence of the Spirit is not the subject in question ; for the consequences would be full of absurdity, if it were to be understood that the Spirit of God was with regard to God, as the spirit of a man is with regard to man. Allusion therefore is made only to the intimate relationship and communion of the Spirit with God, from whom he originally proceeded. That no doubt may remain as to the truth of this interpretation, the following verse is of the same import : ' we have received the Spirit which is of God.' That which is *of* God, cannot be actually God, who is unity. The Son himself disallows the omniscience of the Spirit still more plainly. Matt. xi. 27, ' No man knoweth the Son, but the Father, neither knoweth any man the Father, save the Son, and he to whomsoever the Son will reveal him.' What then becomes of the Holy Spirit ? for according to this passage, no third person whatever knoweth either the Father or the Son, except through their medium. Mark xiii. 32, ' of that day and that hour knoweth no man, no, not the angels which are in heaven, neither the Son, but the Father.' If not even the Son himself, who is also in heaven, then certainly not the Spirit of the Son, who receiveth all things from the Son himself : John xvi. 14.

Secondly, Omnipresence, on the ground that 'the Spirit of God dwelleth in us.' But even if it filled with its presence the whole circle of the earth, with all the heavens, that is, the entire fabric of this world, it would not follow that the Spirit is omnipresent. For why should not the Spirit easily fill with the influence of its power, what the Sun fills with its light; though it does not necessarily follow that we are to believe it infinite? If that lying spirit, I Kings xxii. 22, were able to fill four hundred prophets at once, how many thousands ought we not to think the Holy Spirit capable of pervading, even without the attributes of infinity or immensity?

Thirdly, divine works. Acts ii. 4, 'the Spirit gave them utterance.'; xiii. 2, 'the Holy Ghost said, Separate me Barnabas and Saul for the work.' Acts xx. 28, 'the Holy Ghost hath made you overseers to feed the church of God.' II Pet. i. 21, 'holy men of God spake as they were moved by the Holy Ghost.' A single remark will suffice for the solution of all these passages, if it be only remembered what was the language of Christ respecting the Holy Spirit, the Comforter; namely, that he was sent by the Son from the Father, that he spake not of himself, nor in his own name, and consequently that he did not act in his own name; therefore that he did not even move others to speak of his own power, but that what he gave he had himself received.

Again, I Cor. xii. 11, the Spirit is said 'to divide to every man severally as he will.' In answer to this it may be observed, that the Spirit himself is also said to be divided to each according to the will of God the Father, Heb. ii. 4, and that even 'the wind bloweth where it listeth.' John iii. 8. With regard to the annunciation made to Joseph and Mary, that the Holy Spirit was the author of the miraculous conception, [*conceptionis illius sanctae*] Matt. i. 18, 20. Luke i. 35, it is not to be understood with reference to his own person alone. For it is certain that, in the Old Testament, under the name of the Spirit of God, or of the Holy Spirit, either God the Father himself, or his divine power was signified; nor had Joseph and Mary at that time heard anything of any other Holy Spirit, inasmuch as the personality and divinity of the Holy Spirit are not acknowledged by the Jews even to the present day. Accordingly, in both the passages quoted, πνεῦμα ἅγιον is without the customary article; or if this be not considered as sufficiently decisive, the angel speaks in a more circumstantial manner in St. Luke: 'the Holy Ghost shall come upon thee, and the power of the Highest shall overshadow thee; therefore that holy thing which shall be born of thee shall be called the Son of God' —that is, of the Father: unless we suppose that there are two Fathers—one Father of the

Son of God, another Father of the Son of man.

Fourthly, divine honours. Matt. xxviii. 19, 'baptizing them in the name of the Father, and of the Son, and of the Holy Ghost.' Here mention is undoubtedly made of three persons; but there is not a word that determines the divinity, or unity, or equality of these three. For we read, Matt. x. 41, John xiii. 20, of receiving a prophet in the name of a prophet, and a righteous man in the name of a righteous man, and of giving a cup of cold water in the name of a disciple; which evidently means nothing more, than because he is a prophet, or a righteous man, or a disciple. Thus too the Israelites 'were baptized unto Moses,' I Cor. x. 2, that is, unto the law or doctrine of Moses; and 'unto the baptism of John' occurs in the same sense, Acts xix. 3, and 'in the name of Jesus Christ for the remission of sins,' Acts ii. 38, and 'into Jesus Christ' and 'into his death,' Rom. vi. 3, and 'into one body,' I Cor. xii. 13. To be baptized therefore *in their name*, is to be admitted to those benefits and gifts which we have received through the Son and the Holy Spirit. Hence St. Paul rejoiced that no one could say he had been baptized in his name, I Cor. i. 13–15. It was not the imputation of making himself God that he feared, but that of affecting greater authority than was suitable to his character. From all which it is clear that when we are baptized in the name of the Father, Son, and Holy

Ghost, this is not done to impress upon our minds the inherent or relative natures of these three persons, but the benefits conferred by them in baptism on those who believe—namely, that our eternal salvation is owing to the Father, our redemption to the Son, and our sanctification to the Spirit. The power of the Father is inherent in himself, that of the Son and the Spirit is received from the Father; for it has been already proved on the authority of the Son, that the Son does everything in the name of the Father, and the Spirit everything in the name of the Father and the Son; and a confirmation of the same truth may be derived from the words immediately preceding the verse under discussion; Matt. xxviii. 18, 19, 'all power is given unto me . . . go ye therefore . . . baptizing in the name,' etc., and still more plainly by I Cor. vi. 11, 'but ye are washed, but ye are sanctified, but ye are justified in the name of the Lord Jesus, and by the Spirit of our God.' Here the same three are mentioned as in baptism, 'the Son,' 'the Spirit,' and 'our God'; it follows therefore that the Father alone is our God, of whom are both the Son and the Spirit.

But invocation is made to the Spirit. II Cor. xiii. 14, 'the grace of the Lord Jesus Christ, and the love of God, and the communion of the Holy Ghost, be with you all.' This, however, is not so much an invocation as a benediction, in which the Spirit is not addressed as a person, but sought as a gift, from him who alone is there called God, namely, the Father, from whom Christ himself directs us to seek the communication of the Spirit. Luke xi. 13. If the Spirit were ever to be invoked personally, it would be then especially, when we pray for him; yet we are commanded not to ask him of himself, but only of the Father. Why do we not call upon the Spirit himself, if he be God, to give himself to us? He who is sought from the Father, and given by him, not by himself, can neither be God, nor an object of invocation. The same form of benediction occurs, Gen. xlviii. 15, 16, 'the God before whom my fathers did walk . . . the angel which redeemed me from all evil, bless the lads'; and Rev. i. 4, 'grace be unto you and peace from him which is   and from the seven Spirits.' It is clear that in this passage the seven spirits, of whom more will be said hereafter, are not meant to be invoked. Besides that in this benediction the order or dignity of the things signified should be considered, rather than that of the persons; for it is by the Son that we come to the Father, from whom finally the Holy Spirit is sent. So I Cor. xii. 4–6, 'there are diversities of gifts, but the same Spirit: and there are differences of administrations, but the same Lord: and there are diversities of operations, but it is the same God which worketh all in all.' Here the three are again mentioned in

an inverse order ; but it is one God which worketh
all in all, even in the Son and the Spirit, as we are
taught throughout the whole of Scripture.

Hence it appears that what is said, Matt. xii.
31, 32, has no reference to the personality of the
Holy Spirit. For if to sin against the Holy Spirit
were worse than to sin against the Father and
Son, and if that alone were an unpardonable sin,
the Spirit truly would be greater than the Father
and the Son. The words must therefore apply
to that illumination which, as it is highest in
degree, so it is last in order of time, whereby the
Father enlightens us through the Spirit, and
which if any one resist, no method of salvation
remains open to him. I am inclined to believe,
however, that it is the Father himself who is
here called the Holy Spirit, by whose ' Spirit,'
v. 28, or ' finger,' Luke xi. 20, Christ professed
to cast out devils; when therefore the Pharisees
accused him falsely of acting in concert with
Beelzebub, they are declared to sin unpardonably,
because they said of him who had the Spirit of
his Father, ' he hath an unclean spirit,' Mark
iii. 30. Besides, it was to the Pharisees that he
spoke thus, who acknowledged no other Spirit
than the Father himself. If this be the true
interpretation of the passage, which will not be
doubted by any one who examines the whole
context from v. 24 to v. 32, that dreaded sin
against the Holy Spirit will be in reality a sin

against the Father, who is the Spirit of holiness; of which he would be guilty, who should affirm that the Spirit of the Father which was working in Christ was the prince of the devils, or an unclean spirit;—as Mark clearly shows in the passage quoted above.

But the Spirit bestows grace and blessing upon the churches in conjunction with the Father and the Son: Rev. i. 4, 5, 'grace be unto you and peace from him which is   and from the seven Spirits which are before his throne, and from Jesus Christ.' It is clear, however, that the Holy Spirit is not here meant to be implied; the number of the spirits is inconsistent with such a supposition, as well as the place which they are said to occupy, standing like angels before the throne. See also iv. 5 and v. 6, where the same spirits are called 'seven lamps of fire burning before the throne,' and the 'seven horns' and 'seven eyes' of the Lamb. Those who reduce these spirits to one Holy Spirit, and consider them as synonymous with his sevenfold grace (an opinion which is deservedly refuted by Beza), ought to beware, lest, by attributing to mere virtues the properties of persons, they furnish arguments to those commentators who interpret the Holy Spirit as nothing more than the virtue and power of the Father. This may suffice to convince us, that in this kind of three-fold enumerations the sacred writers have no view whatever to the doctrine of three divine persons, or to the equality or order of those persons;—not even in that verse which has been mentioned above, and on which commentators in general lay so much stress, I John v. 7, 'there are three that bear record in heaven, the Father, the Word, and the Holy Ghost, and these three are one,' where there is in reality nothing which implies either divinity or unity of essence. As to divinity, God is not the only one who is said to bear record in heaven; I Tim. v. 21, 'I charge thee before God, and the Lord Jesus Christ, and the elect angels,'—where it might have been expected that the Holy Spirit would have been named in the third place, if such ternary forms of expression really contained the meaning which is commonly ascribed to them. What kind of unity is intended, is sufficiently plain from the next verse, in which 'the spirit, the water, and the blood' are mentioned, which 'are to bear record to one,' or 'to that one thing.' Beza himself, who is generally a staunch defender of the Trinity, understands the phrase *unum sunt* to mean, 'agree in one.' What it is that they testify, appears in the fifth and sixth verses—namely, that 'he that overcometh the world is he that believeth that Jesus is the Son of God, even Jesus Christ,' that is, 'the anointed'; therefore he is not one with, nor equal to, him that anointed him. Thus the very record that they bear is inconsistent with the essential unity of the witnesses, which is attempted to be deduced from the passage. For the Word is both Son and Christ, that is, as I say, 'anointed'; and as he is the image, as it were, by which we see God, so is he the word by which we hear him. But if such be his nature, he cannot be essentially one with God, whom no one can see or hear. The same has been already proved, by other arguments, with regard to the Spirit; it follows, therefore, that these three are not one in essence. I say nothing of the suspicion of spuriousness attached to the passage, which is a matter of criticism rather than of doctrine. Further, I would ask whether there is one Spirit that bears record in heaven, and another which bears record in earth, or whether both are the same Spirit. If the same, it is extraordinary that we nowhere else read of his bearing witness in heaven, although his witness has always been most conspicuously manifested in earth, that is, in our hearts. Christ certainly brings forward himself and his Father as the only witnesses of himself, John viii. 16, 19. Why then, in addition to two other perfectly competent witnesses, should the Spirit twice bear witness to the same thing? On the other hand, if it be another Spirit, we have here a new and unheard-of doctrine. There are besides other circumstances, which in the opinion of many render the passage suspicious; and yet it is on the authority of this text, almost exclusively, that the whole doctrine of the Trinity has been hastily adopted.

Lest, however, we should be altogether ignorant who or what the Holy Spirit is, although Scripture nowhere teaches us in express terms, it may be collected from the passages quoted above, that the Holy Spirit, inasmuch as he is a minister of God, and therefore a creature, was created or produced of the substance of God, not by a natural necessity, but by the free will of the agent, probably before the foundations of the world were laid, but later than the Son, and far inferior to him. It will be objected that thus the Holy Spirit is not sufficiently distinguished from the Son. I reply that the Scriptural expressions themselves, 'to come forth,' 'to go out from the Father,' 'to proceed from the Father,' which mean the same in the Greek, do not distinguish the Son from the Holy Spirit, inasmuch as these terms are used indiscriminately with reference to both persons, and signify their mission, not their nature. There is, however, sufficient reason for placing the name as well as the nature of the Son above that of the Holy Spirit in the discussion of topics relative to the Deity; inasmuch as the brightness of the glory of God and the express image of his person are said to have been impressed on the one, and not on the other.

The Books in this Catalogue are sold at NET prices. Cheque or Postal Order required with all orders. The Books may be ordered through any Bookseller: this will save cost of carriage. Messrs. Simpkin, Marshall & Co., Ltd., supply Country Booksellers.

Catalogue of Publications

Essex Hall, Essex Street, Strand, London, W.C.

AMES, Charles Gordon, D.D.

The Fatherhood of God, The Brotherhood of Man, Salvation by Character. 1/- net, postage 2d.

ARMSTRONG, Richard A., B.A.

Agnosticism and Theism in the Nineteenth Century. An Historical Study of Religious Thought in England. 2/- net, postage 3d.

Back to Jesus. 1/- net, postage 2d.

God and the Soul: an Essay towards Fundamental Religion. Fourth edition, cloth, 2/- net, postage 3d.; People's edition, paper covers, 6d. net, postage 2d.

The Significance of the Teaching of Jesus: the Essex Hall Lecture for 1897. 1/- net, postage 1d.

'It has all the qualities we might expect—deep religious feeling, adequate knowledge, grave measured eloquence.'—*Liverpool Post.*

The Trinity and the Incarnation. 2/- net, postage 3d.

CONTENTS:—Part I. The Growth of the Doctrine of the Deity of Christ. Part II. Modern Pleas for the Doctrine of the Trinity and the Deity of Christ. Part III. The Heart of the Argument.

Richard Acland Armstrong: Memoir by his son George G. Armstrong, and Selected Sermons, with an Introductory Letter by Philip H. Wicksteed. Photogravure Portrait, 5/- net, postage 4d.

AUTHORITY IN RELIGIOUS BELIEF. 2/- net, postage 3d.

This volume contains twelve essays by various writers, and is issued from a desire to strengthen man's faith in the essential and abiding things of religion.

CONTENTS:—I. Authority in Religious Belief, by Lawrence P. Jacks II. An Introduction to Unitarianism, by Samuel M. Crothers. III. Five Principles of the Liberal Faith, by Charles W. Casson. IV. Salvation: what it is, and is not, by H. W. Crosskey. V. The Ultimate Authority in Religion, by John Page Hopps. VI. How to make the Best of Sunday, by Brooke Herford. VII. Unitarianism an Affirmative Faith, by Charles J. Perry. VIII. The Virgin Birth, by Charles Travers. IX. The Knowledge of God, by Richard W. Boynton. X. Eternal Punishment, by Stopford A. Brooke. XI. Immortal Life, by Theodore Parker. XII. Where to find God, by Frank Walters.

BEACH, Seth Curtis

Daughters of the Puritans. A Group of Brief Biographies, with Portraits. 3/6 net, postage 4d.

CONTENTS:—Catherine Maria Sedgwick, Mary Lovell Ware, Lydia Maria Child, Dorothea Lynde Dix, Sarah Margaret Fuller Ossoli, Harriet Beecher Stowe, Louisa May Alcott.

BEARD, Charles, B.A., LL.D.

Martin Luther and the Reformation in Germany until the close of the Diet of Worms. 5/- net, postage 5d.

The Reformation of the Sixteenth Century in its Relation to Modern Thought and Knowledge. People's edition, 6d. net, postage 2d.

BIRRELL, Augustine

Emerson: A Study of his Life and Influence. 1/- net, postage 2d.

BIXBY, James T., Ph.D.

Similarities of Physical and Religious Knowledge. 1/- net, postage 3d.

The New World and the New Thought. 3/6 net, postage 4d.

BONET-MAURY, Gaston, D.D.

Early Sources of English Unitarian Christianity. Translated by E. P. Hall, Preface by Dr. Martineau. 2/6 net, postage 3d.

BOWIE, W. Copeland (compiled by)

Handbook for Ministers of Religion. Services of Baptism, Dedication, Communion, Marriage, and Burial, with Hymns and Readings. 2/- net, postage 2d.

Seven Services for Public Worship. With Special Prayers and Thanksgivings. 1/- net, postage 2d. [Special terms to congregations ordering quantities.] Musical Responses for Book of Seven Services. Arranged by John M. Bentley. 3d. net, or 2/6 per doz.

Hymns of the Liberal Faith. Fifty-nine Hymns with Tunes. Cloth, 6d. net, Paper covers, 3d. net, postage 2d.; words only, Cloth, 2d. net, Paper covers, 1d., postage 1d.

Record Book and Register of the Congregation. Cloth, 10½ by 8¼, 144 pp. 2/6 net, postage 4d.

Pages are allotted to a Summary of the Trust Deed, Names and Addresses of Trustees, Inventory of Property belonging to the Congregation, Rules, Ministers, Secretaries, Treasurers, Committees, with the dates of their appointment, Anniversaries, Summaries of Income and Expenditure, important Dates and Events in Congregational History.. Fifty pages are provided for the Names and Addresses of the Congregation.

BROOKE, Stopford A., M.A., LL.D.

The Development of Theology, as illustrated in English Poetry from 1780 to 1830. 1/- net, postage 2d.

Jesus and Modern Thought. 9d. net, postage 1d.
Four discourses on the Humanity of Jesus, and the Love we bear to Jesus.

Religion in Literature and in Life. 1/- net, postage 2d.

CARPENTER, J. Estlin, M.A., D.D., D.Litt.

James Martineau, Theologian and Teacher: A Study of his Life and Thought, with two Photogravure Portraits. Second Issue, with Index. 7s. 6d. net., postage 5d.

The First Three Gospels: their Origin and Rela. tions. With a New Chapter on the Historical Value of the Gospels. Cloth, 3s. 6d. net, postage 4d. People's edition, paper covers, 6d. net, postage 3d.

This book is reissued, with some modifications, in the belief that it will supply to some of those who approach the New Testament without technical aid the outlines of a method of literary and historical inquiry into the sources of the life of Jesus.

CARPENTER, J. Estlin, M.A., D.D., D.Litt.—*continued.*

The Place of Christianity in the Religions of the World and other Essays on Comparative Religion. 2/- net, postage 3d.

The Relation of Jesus to his Age and our own. 1/- net, postage 2d.

CHADWICK, John W.

Life of William Ellery Channing. 5/- net, postage 4d.

CHANNING, W. E., D.D.

Select Discourses and Essays. With an Introduction by W. Copeland Bowie. 2/6 net, postage 4d.

The Perfect Life. Twelve Discourses. Paper covers, 6d. net; cloth boards, 1/6 net; postage 3d.

CLARKE, James Freeman, D.D.

Materialism and Atheism Examined. With an Introduction by Sydney H. Mellone, M.A., D.Sc. Paper covers, 6d. net; cloth boards, 1/- net; postage 3d.

CONTENTS:—I. How do we know that we have a Soul? or, Materialism and Immaterialism. II. Why do we believe in God? or, The Evidences of Theism. III. The Atheist's Theory of the Universe. IV. Imperfect and Perfect Theism.

COLLYER, Robert, Litt. D.

Father Taylor. 2/- net, postage 3d.

Father Taylor was the founder of the Seamen's Bethel in the Port of Boston, whose story is here briefly told by Dr. Collyer with a fund of incident and anecdote that well illustrates the peculiar genius and unusual personality of the man.

Where the Light Dwelleth. Twenty Sermons. With a Photogravure Portrait. Biographical Sketch by Charles Hargrove, M.A. Cloth, gilt top, 3/6 net; French morocco, full gilt back and edges, 5/- net, postage 4d.

COMMON-SENSE THEOLOGY. 2/- net, postage 3d.

CREED OR CONSCIENCE? Twelve Essays by various writers. 2/- net, postage 3d.

CROOKER, Joseph H., D.D.

New Testament Views of Jesus. 6d. net, postage 1d.

The Supremacy of Jesus. 3/- net, postage 4d.

CONTENTS:—I. The Historic Position of Jesus. II. Jesus and Gospel Criticism. III. A New Appreciation of Jesus. IV. The Master of Inner Life. V. The Authority of Jesus.

CROOKER, Joseph H., D.D.—*continued.*
The Church of To-Day. 2/6 net, postage 3d.
'A remarkably well written, well considered, well reasoned "plea" for the due appreciation of "the church" as an organization naturally fitted to meet human needs that are fundamental and universal; an essential factor in the corporate life of communities, and to-day not less but more needed than ever.'—*Chicago Tribune.*

CROSSKEY, H. W., LL.D., F.G.S.
A Handbook of Rational Piety. 1/- net, postage 3d.

CROTHERS, Samuel McChord, D.D.
The Making of Religion. 1/- net, postage 2d.
The Understanding Heart. 2/6 net, postage 3d.
CONTENTS:—I. Methods of Teaching. II. The Sense of Values. III. Symbols. IV. Literature and Morals. V. Work and Worship. VI. The Higher Intelligence. VII. Moral Discipline. VIII. On the Study of the Bible. IX. Our Historic Inheritance. X. How Religion is organizing itself.

DAVIS, V. D., B.A., Edited by
A Book of Daily Strength. Selections from Unitarian Writers for every day in the year. Cloth, 3/6 net, postage 4d.; leather, extra gilt, 5/- net, postage 3d.

DELITZSCH, Prof. Friedrich
Whose Son is Christ? Two Lectures on Progress in Religion. Translated by F. L. Pogson, M.A. 1/6 net, postage 2d.
The author holds that Protestantism, when possessed of a full consciousness of its sacred task of serving the truth, will free the life and teaching of Jesus from the dross which has collected on both and threatened to smother them.

DOGMA OR DOCTRINE? 2/- net, postage 3d.
CONTENTS:—Dogma or Doctrine? by J. M. Lloyd Thomas; Science and Religion, by W. B. Carpenter; The Religion of 'Robert Falconer,' by Alex. Webster; The Revolt against Calvinism, by Alex. Webster; Theology and Miracle, by Stopford A. Brooke; Trinity Sunday, by Charles Beard; God the Father the only intelligible object of Worship, by H. W. Bellows; A Rational View of the Bible, by C. J. Street; Jesus Christ, by Brooke Herford; The Blood of Christ, by Silas Farrington; Rationalism: what it is and what it is not, by Frank Walters; The Covenant of the Spirit, by James Drummond.

DRUMMOND, James, M.A., LL.D.
Studies in Christian Doctrine. 10/6 net, postage 5d.
The Contents include the following:—The Rights and Limitations of the Intellect; The Moral Nature and Revelation; The Religious Element in Man; The Bible; The Church; Primary Conceptions of God; The Doctrine of the Trinity; Agency and Attributes of God; Doctrine of Man; Reconciliation; The Person of Christ; The Work of Christ; Means of Grace; Rise and Progress of Religion in the Individual.

DRUMMOND, James, M.A., LL.D.—*continued.*

The Pauline Benediction.   1/- net, postage 2d.

CONTENTS :—I. The Grace of Christ; II. The Love of God ; III. The Communion of the Holy Spirit.

Some Thoughts on Christology : the Essex Hall Lecture for 1902.   1/- net, postage 2d.

DRUMMOND, Robert B., B.A.

The Christology of the New Testament.   Five Expository Discourses.   1/- net, postage 2d.

This little book makes no pretension to anything like a systematic or adequate treatment of the subject named on its title page. Its aim is merely to throw light on one or two special points of interest, and to explain, from the point of view of modern criticism, a few of the most disputed texts of the New Testament.

ELIOT, Charles W., LL.D.

Four American Leaders.   2/- net, postage 3d.

This volume contains four essays on Franklin, Washington, Channing, and Emerson, condensed in expression and broad in suggestiveness. They summarize the influence of these great Americans in shaping the political, moral, and intellectual trend of the Republic, and by their lives and writings in framing American ideals.

EMERSON, Ralph Waldo

Divinity School Address.   With an Introduction and Portrait.   1/- net, postage 2d.

ESSEX HALL HYMNAL REVISED (1902)

In Small Pica, 534 Hymns, cloth, red edges, size 6¾ by 4¼ by 1¼ inches, 1/6 net, postage 4d.   Congregations ordering at least 20 copies supplied direct from the publishers, *not through the Trade*, at a reduction.

ESSEX HALL CHANT BOOK

Containing 97 Psalms and Canticles, Doxologies, etc., pointed for Chanting.   Cloth, 6d. net, postage 2d.

ESSEX HALL YEAR BOOK

A List of Unitarian, Free Christian, Presbyterian, and other Non-subscribing Churches, with names and addresses of Ministers and Secretaries, Missionary Societies, Colleges, Trust Funds, etc. Published in January.   1/- net, postage 2d.

FORREST, James, M.A. (Formerly McQuaker Lecturer).

Religion and the Scientific Spirit.   1/- net, postage 2d.

CONTENTS :—1. Modern Views of Bible Inspiration.   2. Science and the Bible.   3. Science and God.   4. Science and Sin.   5. The Christ of the Liberal Faith.   6. Christian Principles and Social Problems.

FOX, William Johnson

The Religious Ideas. Fifteen Lectures, with a brief biographical sketch. Paper covers, 6d. net, postage 2d.; cloth boards, 1/6 net, postage 3d.

'We would earnestly commend this little book to the attention of teachers and inquirers. . . . . It is not a manual of Unitarianism or any ism, but an earnest attempt to make clear the foundations on which all religions are built up.'—*The Inquirer*.

FREE CHURCH, THE FAITH OF A 2/- net, postage 3d.

CONTENTS:—The Faith of a Free Church, by S. M. Crothers; The Religion the Age Wants, by S. Fletcher Williams; What is a Unitarian Christian? by H. W. Crosskey; The Jesus of the Gospels and the Jesus of History, by J. E. Carpenter; The Church, the Bible, and Free Thought, by Charles Beard; The Revolt from Calvinism within Scotch Churches, by Alex. Webster; Theism in India, by Pundit Sivanath N. Sastri; The Brahmo Samaj of India: A Statement of its Religious Principles; Search the Scriptures, by W. Copeland Bowie; The God-Christ or the Human Christ? by R. A. Armstrong.

FREEDOM AND FELLOWSHIP IN RELIGION. Proceedings and Papers of the Fourth International Congress of Religious Liberals held at Boston, U.S.A., with Sixty Portraits. Edited by Charles W. Wendté. 5/- net, postage 6d.

GANNETT, William C.

The Christmas Birth-Poem. 6d. net, postage 1d.

GORDON, Alexander, M.A.

Heads of English Unitarian History, with Lectures on Richard Baxter and Dr. Priestley. 1/- net, postage 3d.

GOSPEL OF THE BETTER HOPE. 1/- net, postage 3d.

GREG, Samuel

Short Sermons. 1/- net, postage 3d.

CONTENTS:—Angels; Sunshine; The Temptation; The Box of Ointment; The One Talent; A Living Sacrifice; Almost and Altogether; Lost Opportunities; Christianity a Spirit, not a Law; Character changed by Circumstances; Wishing is not Willing; The Voices of the Dead; Six Prayers.

HARDY, Thomas J., B.A.

A Confession of Heresy and a Plea for Frankness. 1/- net, postage 1d.

HARGROVE, Charles, M.A.

Jesus of Nazareth. Lessons of his Life, Death, and Resurrection, learnt at Ober Ammergau. 1/- net, postage 2d.

8   *BOOKS OF LIBERAL RELIGION*

HERFORD, Brooke, D.D.
   Anchors of the Soul. A Volume of Sermons. With a Biographical Sketch by Philip H. Wicksteed, M.A. 5/- net, postage 4d.
   Courage and Cheer. Second edition, with Portrait. 2/6 net, postage 4d.
   Eutychus. Pulpit and Pew Papers. 2/- net, postage 2d.
   Religious Thought as interpreted by Unitarians. 1/- net, postage 3d.

HOME PAGES
   Edited by Helen Brooke Herford. 1/- net, postage 2d.
   CONTENTS:—(1) Woman's Work and Care, by Brooke Herford, D.D.; (2) Jem Cooper's Geraniums, by E. Baumer Williams; (3) Patchwork, by Brooke Herford, D.D.; (4) 'A Bit On,' by J. Crowther Hirst; (5) In Honour Preferring One Another, by Brooke Herford, D.D.; (6) A Preacher's Message, by Frances E. Cooke; (7) A World without Worship; (8) Blessed be Drudgery, by W. C. Gannett; (9) 'Early will I seek Thee'; (10) Yes and No, by J. J. Wright; (11) Where is thy God? by Brooke Herford, D.D.; (12) Nicodemus, by Brooke Herford, D.D.

IERSON, Henry, M.A.
   Notes on the Amended English Bible, with reference to certain texts in the Revised Version, bearing upon the principles of Unitarian Christianity. 1/- net, postage 3d.

JONES, Henry, LL.D., D.Litt.
   The immortality of the Soul in the Poems of Tennyson and Browning. 1/- net, postage 2d.
   'The Lecture is a brilliant addition to the ever-increasing literature of the great Victorian poets.'—*Scotsman.*

JUPP, W. J.
   The Religion of Nature and of Human Experience. 2/- net, postage 3d.
   CONTENTS:—Chapter I. Prelude. II. The Kinship of Nature. III. The Return to Nature. IV. The Healing Grace of Nature. V. Pioneers of the Religion of Nature. VI. Seer and Poet. VII. The Witness of Science. VIII. The Poet Naturalist (1). IX. The Poet Naturalist (2). X. The Appeal of Beauty. XI. The Ethical Ideal. XII. The Faith of the Religion of Nature. XIII. Human Fellowship in the Religion of Nature.

KRÜGER, Prof. Dr. Gustav
   Dogma and History. 1/- net, postage 2d.
   Intended for those who have little acquaintance with the historical development of religious ideas, and especially for those who, while becoming ever more uncertain about the validity of Creeds and Dogmas, cannot see their way to true religion without them.

LAMSON, Alvan, D.D.
   The Church of the First Three Centuries. Notices of some of the Early Fathers, with special reference to the Doctrine of the Trinity. 2/- net, postage 4d.

LIBERAL RELIGIOUS THOUGHT AT THE BEGIN-NING OF THE TWENTIETH CENTURY

Essays and Addresses dealing with the Condition and Pro-spects of Liberal Religion in Europe and America. Edited by W. Copeland Bowie. 1/6 net, postage 3d.

LLOYD, Walter

A Theist's Apology. A Reply to Agnosticism. 1/- net, postage 2d.

CONTENTS:—I. Agnosticism. II. Religious Agnosticism. III. Evil. IV. The Knowledge of God. V. Faith. VI. The Ethical Struggle. VII. Beneficence. VIII. God and the World. IX. Religion.

The Story of Protestant Dissent and English Unitarianism. 2/6 net, postage 4d.

CONTENTS:—I. Introduction. II. The Presbyterians. III. Richard Baxter. IV. The Ejection, 1662. V. The Protestant Dissenters, 1689. VI. The Meeting-Houses. VII. Non-Subscription. VIII. The 'Christians Only.' IX. The Unitarians. X. John Biddle. XI. Lindsey, Priestley, and Belsham. XII. The Unitarian Societies. XIII. The Trinitarian Controversy. XIV. Undogmatic Unitarianism. XV. Conclusion.

McQUAKER LECTURES, 1890

Free Thought and Christian Faith. 1/- net, postage 3d.

CONTENTS:—(1) Rationalism: what it is and what it is not, by Frank Walters; (2) The Place of Jesus of Nazareth in Modern Religion, by R. A. Armstrong, B.A.; (3) What is a Unitarian Christian? by H. W. Crosskey, LL.D., F.G.S.; (4) The Limits of Compromise in the Profession of Faith, by C. Hargrove, M.A.

McQUAKER LECTURES, 1892

Old and New Conceptions. 1/- net, postage 3d.

CONTENTS:—(1) Old and New Conceptions of the Structure and Chronology of the Old Testament, by P. H. Wicksteed, M.A.; (2) The Jesus of the Gospels and the Jesus of History, by J. E. Carpenter, M.A.; (3) Incarnations of God, by John Page Hopps.

MARTINEAU, James, LL.D., D.C.L., D.D.

Endeavours after the Christian Life. (2 vols.) With brief introduction. Paper covers, 6d. each net; cloth, superior paper, with portrait, 1/6 each net, postage 3d.

MAY, Joseph, LL.D

Miracles and Myths of the New Testament. 1/6 net, postage 2d.

CONTENTS:—I. The New Testament Miracles. II. The Origin of belief in Miracles. III. The Myth of the Resurrection of Jesus. IV. The Myth of the Deity of Jesus. V. Jesus as he was.

MELLONE, Sydney H., M.A., D.Sc.
Converging Lines of Religious Thought. 2/- net,
postage 3d.
CONTENTS:—Introduction; Belief in God; Revelation, Inspiration,
and Miracle; The Incarnation and the Trinity; The Atonement, Redemption, and Education; The Immortal Hope; Notes.

MEMORABLE UNITARIANS. Brief Biographies of 150
eminent Unitarians. 1/- net, postage 4d.

**MILTON ON THE SON OF GOD AND THE HOLY
SPIRIT.** (From his treatise on 'Christian Doctrine.')
With an Introduction by Alexander Gordon, M.A. 1/6 net,
postage 3d.

MOTT, Frederick Blount
A Short History of Unitarianism. 1/- net, postage 2d.
CONTENTS:—Chapter I. The Pursuit of Truth. II. Bernardino Ochino.
III. Servetus the Martyr. IV. Fausto Sozzini. V. The Strangers' Church.
VI. John Bidle. VII. Theophilus Lindsey. VIII. Joseph Priestley.
IX. Beginnings in America. X. William Ellery Channing. XI. Emerson's
New Seed. XII. Theodore Parker. XIII. James Martineau. XIV. The
Unitarian Faith.

NEWMAN, Francis William
Morning Prayers in the Household of a Believer in
God. 1/- net, postage 2d.
The Soul, its Sorrows and its Aspirations. Memoir
and Introduction by C. B. Upton, B.A., B.Sc. 2/6 net, post-
age 4d. People's edition, paper covers, 6d. net, postage 3d.

ODGERS, James Edwin, M.A., D.D.
The Teaching of the Twelve Apostles for English
Readers. A Translation with Introduction and Notes.
Cloth, 1/- net, postage 2d.; paper covers, 6d. net, post-
age 1d.

OSLER, Mrs. A. C.
Life's Upper School. The discipline of adversity and
sorrow. Cloth, 9d. net; paper covers, 4d. net, postage 1d.

OUTER AND INNER WORLD. 1/- net, postage 3d.
SERMONS by James Martineau, LL.D., D.D., D.C.L., H. Enfield Dowson,
B.A., V. D. Davis, B.A., A. N. Blatchford, B.A., J. E. Manning, M.A.,
S. A. Steinthal, Frank Walters, D. Walmsley, B.A., H. Woods Perris,
C. H. Wellbeloved, Joseph Wood, C. C. Coe, F.R.G.S.

PARKER, Theodore
Experience as a Minister, with some account of his Early
Life and Education for the Ministry. 6d. net, postage 2d.

PERRY, Charles John, B.A.
Spiritual Perspective, and other Sermons. Second
edition. 1/6 net, postage 3d.

PIERCE, Ulysses G. B.
The Soul of the Bible. Selected passages from the Old and New Testaments and the Apocrypha arranged as synthetic readings in Biblical order, with an Introduction by Dr. Edward Everett Hale. Cloth, 3/- net, postage 4d. Thin paper, cloth, gilt top, 3/6 net; flexible leather, red under gilt edges, 5/- net, postage 3d.

POSITIVE ASPECTS OF UNITARIAN CHRISTIANITY.
Preface by Dr. James Martineau. 1/- net, postage 3d.

PRIESTLEY, Joseph, LL.D., F.R.S.
A History of the Corruptions of Christianity. 2/- net, postage 3d.

PRITCHARD, Marian
The Poem of Job. With Introduction and Notes. Paper covers, 6d. net, postage 2d.; cloth boards, 1/- net, postage 3d.

RELIGION AND LIBERTY.
Addresses and Essays at the second International Council of Unitarian and other Liberal Religious Thinkers, at Amsterdam. 2/- net, postage 4d.

RELIGION AND LIFE. 1/- net, postage 3d.

RELIGION AND MODERN THOUGHT. 2/-net, postage 3d.

RELIGION AND THEOLOGY OF UNITARIANS.
2/- net, postage 3d.

CONTENTS:—Seeking God and Finding Him, by J. E. Manning ; Was Jesus God? by J. T. Sunderland ; Eternal Punishment, by G. Vance Smith ; Where did the Bible come from? by J. Page Hopps ; The Person of Christ, by William Gaskell ; Main Lines of Unitarianism, by Brooke Herford ; What do Unitarians Believe? by Charles Hargrove ; Christianity and Social Problems, by Stopford A. Brooke ; Unitarian Christianity and Citizenship, by John Dendy ; Unitarian Churches in the British Isles, by W. Copeland Bowie ; Religion of Oliver Wendell Holmes, by W. G. Tarrant ; The Eternal Goodness and The Minister's Daughter, Two Poems by John Greenleaf Whittier

RÉVILLE, Albert, D.D.
History of the Dogma of the Deity of Jesus Christ. A Revised Translation from the third French edition of 1904. 2/6 net, postage 4d.

The volume deals first with the formation of the Dogma of the Deity of Jesus Christ from the earliest days of Christianity to the commencement of the Middle Ages ; then with the absolute domination of the dogma from the commencement of the Middle Ages to the Eve of the Reformation ; and finally with the continuous decline of the dogma from the Reformation to our own days.

RIX, Herbert, B.A.

Rabbi, Messiah, Martyr. A Modern Picture of the Story of Jesus. 1/- net, postage 2d.

The author of these short sketches of the life of Jesus here sets forth, as clearly and definitely as possible, a picture of the great Life as it emerges in our day, freed from the dust and distortions of tradition.

SADLER, Thomas, Ph.D.

Addresses, Prayers, and Hymns. 1/- net, postage 2d.

Sunday Thoughts at Rosslyn Hill. 2/6 net, postage 4d.

SAVAGE, Minot J., D.D.

Men and Women. 3/- net, postage 4d.

Pillars of the Temple. 3/6 net, postage 4d.

CONTENTS:—I. The God we worship. II. The Christ we love. III. The Heaven we hope for. IV. The Hell we fear. V. The Bible we accept. VI. The Divine Inspiration. VII. The Salvation we Believe in. VIII. The Church we belong to.

The Passing and the Permanent in Religion. People's edition. Paper covers, 6d. net, postage 2d.

CONTENTS:—The Universe, Man, Bibles, Gods and God, Saviours, Worship, Prayer.

SERMONS BY UNITARIAN MINISTERS. First Series.

Twelve Sermons on Practical Religion. 1/6 net, postage 3d.

CONTENTS:—The Unseen Things in Life, by R. A. Armstrong, B.A.; The Besetting God, by C. J. Street, M.A., LL.B.; Hidden Treasure, by W. G. Tarrant, B.A.; Religion and Historical Theology, by R. T. Herford, B.A.; The Divine Tenderness, by Frank Walters; Overcoming Evil, by J. Worsley Austin, M.A.; The Sufficing Joy, by W. J. Jupp; The Revival of Mysticism, by J. M. Lloyd Thomas; Drifting, by Ambrose Bennett, M.A.; The Perfection of the Heart, by W. Whitaker, B.A.; Humanized Religion, by Alex. Webster; Things to Live for, by Charles Roper, B.A.

SERMONS BY UNITARIAN MINISTERS. Second Series.

Twelve Sermons on Practical Religion. 1/6 net, postage 3d.

CONTENTS:—The Sense of Wonder, by Joseph Wood; Pharisee and Publican, by Henry Gow, B.A.; The Witness of the Spirit, by E. D. Priestley Evans; Spiritual Religion, by A. W. Fox, M.A.; The Parable of the Talents, by W. Wooding, B.A.; A Revaluation of Values, by J. J. Wright; Ability and Sympathy, by Alfred Hall, M.A.; Love, the True Religion, by Walter Lloyd; The Hours of Sunshine, by H. S. Solly, M.A.; The Shepherd of Souls, by Wilfred Harris, M.A.; Unity not Uniformity, by E. L. H. Thomas, B.A.; The Book of Life, by J. H. Weatherall, M.A.

SMITH, G. Vance, Ph.D., D.D.

Modern Phases of the Atonement. 1/- net, postage 2d.

Texts and Margins of the Revised New Testament. Paper, 3d.; cloth, 1/- net, postage 1d.

SMITH, Goldwin, D.C.L.
The Founder of Christendom. 1/6 net, postage 2d.

SMITH, Southwood, M.D.
The Divine Government. 2/- net, postage 3d.
This book contains a statement of the evidence and reasons for holding the doctrine of the ultimate purity and happiness of all mankind.

SOLLY, Henry Shaen, M.A.
Know Thyself. An attempt to answer certain questions relating to Duty, to God, and to Immortality. 1/- net, postage 3d.

STANNUS, Hugh H.
History of the Origin of the Doctrine of the Trinity. Introduction by Robert Spears. 1/- net, postage 3d.

STREET, Christopher J., M.A., LL.B.
Immortal Life. 1/- net, postage 2d.
Jesus the Prophet of God. 2/- net, postage 3d.
'This is a thoughtful and well-written book, in which the narratives of the Gospels are regarded from the point of view of modern Unitarianism. The treatment is at once bold and reverential.'—*Manchester Guardian.*

SWANWICK, Anna, LL.D.
Evolution and the Religion of the Future. 1/- net, postage 2d.

TARRANT, W. G., B.A.
John Milton: the Man, the Patriot, and the Poet. 1/- net, postage 1d.
Bee Songs, and other Verse. 1/- net. postage 2d.
The Beginnings of Christendom. The formation of the New Testament, rise of the Priesthood and Growth of the Creeds. 1/- net, postage 2d.
Daily Meditations. A Manual of Devotion for morning use. 4th edition. Cloth, 6d. net; leather gilt, 1/- net, postage 1d.
Night unto Night. A Manual of Devotion for evening use. Cloth, 6d. net; leather gilt, 1/- net, postage 1d.
Unitarianism Restated. Four Lectures, 6d. net, postage 1d.

TAYLER, John James, B.A.
Life and Letters of John James Tayler. Edited by John Hamilton Thom. 2/6 net, postage 4d.

THINK FOR YOURSELF. 9d. net, postage 1d.

THOM, J. Hamilton

A Spiritual Faith. Second (abridged) edition. 2/- net, postage 3d.

Laws of Life after the Mind of Christ. 1st Series. New edition. 2/6 net, postage 4d.

Laws of Life after the Mind of Christ. 2nd Series. New edition. 2/6 net, postage 4d.

A Minister of God. Selections from Occasional Sermons and Addresses. Edited with a Memoir by V. D. Davis, B.A. 2/- net, postage 3d.

Christ the Revealer. Discourses and Essays. Third edition. 2/- net, postage 3d.

TRANSIENT AND PERMANENT IN RELIGION. 2/- net, postage 3d.

CONTENTS:—I. The Transient and Permanent in Christianity, by Theodore Parker II. Some Difficulties of Unbelief, by S. Fletcher Williams. III. Principles of Religion, by Amherst D. Tyssen. IV. The Miracles of the Bible, by Walter Lloyd. V. Unitarianism and the 'New Theology,' by S. H. Mellone. VI. The Brotherhood of Man, by C. Gordon Ames. VII. Agnosticism from a Unitarian's Point of View, by Lawrence P. Jacks. VIII. Baptism, by Brooke Herford. IX. The Communion Service, by Brooke Herford. X. The Heretic, by Henry W. Hawkes. XI. Unitarian Leaflets (Nos. 1-12). XII. Questions and Answers.

TRIUMPH OF FAITH. 2/- net, postage 3d.

TYPES OF RELIGIOUS EXPERIENCE. 1/6 net, postage 3d.

CONTENTS:—Anglican to Unitarian; by E. W. Lummis, M.A. Congregationalist to Unitarian; by William Wooding, B.A. Methodist to Unitarian; by G. V. Crook. Presbyterian to Unitarian; by Alexander Webster. Roman Catholic to Unitarian; by L. de Beaumont Klein, D.Sc.

UNITARIAN POCKET BOOK AND DIARY, with List of Ministers and Congregations. Tuck case. Published in December. 1/3 net, postage 1d.

UPTON, Charles B., B.A., B.Sc.

Dr. Martineau's Philosophy of Religion. A Survey. Revised cheap edition, with an Introductory Essay. 3/6 net, postage 4d.

VERITIES OF RELIGION. 1/- net, postage 3d.

Sermons by Revs. J. H. Thom; R. A. Armstrong, B.A.; C. J. Street, M.A.; John Dendy, B.A.; S. F. Williams; John Page Hopps; L. P. Jacks, M.A.; J. E. Carpenter, M.A.; J. E. Odgers, M.A.; W. E. Addis, M.A.; W. Binns; F. K. Freeston.

VIZARD, P. E.

From the Old Faith to the New. 1/- net, postage 3d.

CONTENTS:—(1) The Bible: Inspiration; (2) Miracles; (8) Jesus in Relation to Modern Thought; (4) The Death of Jesus; (5) The Resurrection of Jesus.

Prayers, New and Old. With a brief note on Prayer, a Selection of Collects, and a Table of Bible Readings. Third edition, Revised, 1/6 net, postage 2d.

WARD, Mrs. Humphry

Unitarians and the Future. 1/- net, postage 2d.

WARSCHAUER, J., M.A., D.Phil.

The Problem of the Fourth Gospel. 2/- net, postage 3d.

CONTENTS:—I. The Problem Stated. II. The First Three Gospels and the Fourth. III. The Fourth Gospel as History. IV. Was John the Author? V. Conclusions and Conclusion.

WEBSTER, Alexander

My Pilgrimage from Calvinism to Unitarianism. An account of Spiritual Experience. Fifth edition. 1/- net, postage 2d.

WENDT, Prof. H. H., Ph.D., D.D.

The Idea and Reality of Revelation, and Typical Forms of Christianity. Two Lectures, 1/6 net, postage 2d.

The author shows how all God's workings have the education of mankind as their final end. This end is served by the whole natural world; it is furthered by the mental equipment of man with reason, conscience, freedom; and it is served also by the religious knowledge which God has granted to man in a gradual historical Revelation which finds its fullest expression in Jesus Christ.

WERNLE, Prof. Paul, D.Th.

The Sources of our Knowledge of the Life of Jesus. Translated by E. W. Lummis, M.A. 2/- net, postage 3d.

CONTENTS:—Preface. I. Source Material outside the Four Gospels. II. Our Four Evangelists. III. The Synoptics. IV. The Sources of the Synoptics.

WHAT DO UNITARIANS BELIEVE AND TEACH?

2/- net, postage 3d.

CONTENTS:—1. Brief Statement of Unitarianism; Brooke Herford. 2. Unitarian Christianity Explained; R. A. Armstrong. 3. Plea for Unitarian Christianity; W. Copeland Bowie. 4. What must I do to be Saved? C. J. Street. 5. The Doctrine of the Atonement; James Harwood. 6. The Bible a Human Book; Frank Walters. 7. Modern Biblical Criticism; Crawford H. Toy. 8. Miracles and Modern Knowledge; J. T. Sunderland. 9. Incarnation; W. Channing Gannett. 10. Prayer and Modern Thought; C. Gordon Ames. 11. The Immortal Hope; J. W. Chadwick. 12. Our Unitarian Gospel; M. J. Savage.

ESSEX HALL, ESSEX STREET, STRAND, LONDON, W.C.

CPSIA information can be obtained
at www.ICGtesting.com
Printed in the USA
BVOW09s1153271017

498825BV00022B/1107/P